"Melanie Phillips…provides great insight into the Leftist mindset, exposing their ideology as morally bankrupt and detrimental to Western civilization. Phillips convincingly exposes the logical fallacies inherent in progressive arguments, their motives and the vitriol with which they will fire on any who do not toe the proverbial party line. *Guardian Angel* is a great introduction to one of the most prolific and penetrating polemicists there is on topics ranging from global warming to Islam."

The Blaze

"Melanie Phillips' story is ultimately a reminder that politics is governed by deep emotions that even in the heat of battle deserve to be understood and respected."

Gaby Hinsliff, The Guardian

"Melanie Phillips is the wonder woman of journalism. With powerful pen, incorruptible integrity, and rare courage she identifies what is going wrong and directs the cultural battle against what she is not afraid to call evil. This is her story."

Ruth Wisse, professor of Yiddish Literature, Harvard

T0019436

guardian angel

MY JOURNEY FROM LEFTISM TO SANITY

MELANIE PHILLIPS

BOMBARDIER
BOOKS

A BOMBARDIER BOOKS BOOK
An Imprint of Post Hill Press

ISBN: 978-1-68261-568-3
ISBN (eBook): 978-1-68261-569-0

Guardian Angel
My Journey from Leftism to Sanity
© 2018 by Melanie Phillips

Cover Design by Christian Bentulan

Post Hill Press
New York • Nashville
posthillpress.com
Published in the United States of America

Table of Contents

Introduction

When Britain voted in June 2016 to leave the European Union, the reaction of many who had supported the Remain side in the referendum was quite remarkable.

It wasn't just that they were bad losers. It wasn't just that, having issued blood-curdling warnings of an economic apocalypse, they were now claiming that this had actually come to pass – even while the UK economy, although predictably unsettled, was showing a robust refusal to collapse.

Much more striking was their incandescent rage and incredulity that Britain could possibly have voted in defiance of everything the Remain side had been saying.

According to the Remainers, those who had backed Britain exiting the EU – the Brexiteers, as they were called – simply hadn't understood what they were voting for. The working class, which had astounded the Remainers by voting in huge numbers to leave the EU, was deemed too stupid to have grasped what was at stake. These people, the Remainers claimed, had all voted for Brexit just to stop immigration, thus proving they were so nasty and bigoted that their votes should not be as valid as those cast for liberal, tolerant, outward-looking Remain.

In vain did polling data suggest that, on the contrary, concern over immigration had taken second place to the desire for Britain to control its own policies and laws. In vain was it shown that most people who voted for Brexit were the non-metropolitan middle class.

All this and more was brushed aside. The Remainers seemed to believe that the march of progress itself had been halted and Britain was about to be engulfed by a new dark age – all because people wanted to rule themselves through democratic government embodying their nation's particular history, institutions and culture.

The Remainers lamented that their country had been taken away from them. Strikingly, this was precisely the feeling articulated by many Brexiteers. The difference was that those who wanted to feel that an independent Britain was still their recognizable homeland were correct to think it had been transformed almost beyond recognition. The Remainers, by contrast, had merely lost an argument.

To me, the Remainers' reaction came as no surprise. I was all too familiar with this mindset. For the significance of the Brexit vote went far beyond the immediate issue of EU membership. It represented the defeat of a progressive worldview that had been actively reshaping British and Western culture for more than half a century.

This view was rooted in the belief that the Western nation was the source of global oppression, bigotry and war. It therefore needed to be constrained by transnational institutions such as the EU and the United Nations, and by "universal" laws such as human rights. Because transnationalism embodied the brotherhood of man, these institutions would necessarily supersede national parliaments and their laws.

The belief that the Western nation was innately and oppressively judgmental gave rise to a parallel onslaught against its Judeo-Christian heritage. This great "march through the institutions" captured virtually the entire British intellectual and governing establishment. It led to the undermining of education, the traditional family and behavioral constraints in favor of cultural and moral relativism and hyper-individualism.

To this agenda of cultural transformation, no dissent was permitted. The progressive establishment regarded anyone who questioned this orthodoxy as an enemy of all things decent. There was simply no argument to be had. Any deviation had to be stamped out.

Opponents were demonized, vilified and smeared. Anyone who opposed the progressive consensus was damned as racist, xenophobic, Islamophobic, homophobic, narrow-minded, imbecilic and invariably "right-wing."

In more than fifty years of these culture wars, the progressive establishment in Britain never lost a battle. Until the Brexit vote, that is. On June 23, 2016, the British people found the courage to assert once again the rightfulness and desirability of an independent Western democratic nation giving expression to its own historic culture, beliefs and laws.

That explains the hysteria of the Remain side. For this was not merely an argument about trade deals or migration policy or even the sovereignty of Parliament. The vote was a reassertion of the western nation and its cultural values. It was a stunning defeat for those who were intent on undermining them – and who had assumed any pushback was confined to a few cranks and was therefore simply unthinkable.

A similar pushback took place in the United States with the election as president in November 2016 of Donald J. Trump. Whatever one may think about Trump's character, he was brought to power by a revolt against a political and intellectual establishment which had long sought to erode America's values at home and emasculate its power abroad. The erosion of the rule of law through the systematic toleration of illegal immigration, the espousal of ideological policies on "climate change" which undermined employment and living standards for American workers, the support given by America to the West's mortal enemies such as Iran or the Muslim Brotherhood – these and other policies and attitudes were all based on the core belief that America, as the leader of the Western world, was an innate force for bad whose interests and values should therefore not be defended.

Both in voting for Brexit and for Donald Trump, the people were demanding the upholding of their core culture, the defense of their nation and the restoration of the democratic compact of citizenship with their country's government. On both sides of the Atlantic, however, those who had spent decades progressively undermining the West's core values and powers of national self-government simply refused to accept the repudiation of their worldview. The result was that, in Britain, a fight to the death ensued to negate the Brexit vote through negotiating a deal that would be half-in, half-out of the EU and, in America, to remove Donald Trump from office by fair means or foul.

I have long been associated with fighting these "culture wars" in the defense of western values against their attackers. This memoir, however, is the story of my own culture war: the account of my personal battles with the hate-mongering left.

It is an account of the tumultuous roller coaster of a journey I have been on both in my personal life and my professional career as a journalist. For that is a career in which, having started out in the very belly of the left-wing beast, I have been obsessively denounced for subsequently having abandoned the moral high ground of progressive politics and become instead "right-wing."

This accusation is in fact meaningless, since the left merely deploys the term "right-wing" as a crude insult against anyone who dares challenge its shibboleths. It uses this taunt to shut down debate by bullying its targets and labelling them as extremists, bigots or other enemies of humanity in order to frighten people away from listening to them.

In fact, I have never been fighting these battles from "the right." Instead, I have taken the fight to the left from its very own purported moral high ground, which I once believed we all shared but which I came to realize it had most cynically traduced.

I always believed in the duty of a journalist to uphold truth over lies, follow the evidence where it led and fight abuses of power wherever they were to be found. I gradually realized, however, that the left was not on the side of truth, reason, and justice, but instead promoted ideology, malice, and oppression. Rather than fighting the abuse of power, it embodied it.

Through demonizing its enemies in this way, the left has undermined the possibility of finding common ground and all but destroyed rational discourse. This is because it substitutes insult and abuse for argument and reasoned disagreement.

More devastatingly still, by twisting the meaning of words such as liberal, compassion, justice, and many others into their opposites, it has hijacked the center ground of politics. Left-wing ideology is now falsely said to constitute the moderate center ground, while the true center ground is now vilified as "the right."

This is as mind-bending as it is destructive, for it has introduced a fatal confusion into political debate on both sides of the Atlantic. Redefining the true middle ground of politics as "right-wing" has served to besmirch and toxify the commitment to truth, reason, decency, and reality that characterize where most people happen to situate their thinking. At the same time, by loudly asserting that left-wing ideology is really "centrist," the left has succeeded in presenting extremist, antisocial, or even nihilistic ideas as unarguably good, and all dissent is promptly vilified as "extreme."

The result has been a retreat from reason and a polarization of political debate, with each side circling its wagons and striking ever more inflexible, dogmatic and adversarial positions. What I have been trying to do is to break out of those absurd caricatures to reconnect politics to the world of reality. Despite the epithets hurled my way, I am not "right-wing;" how can I be, when I am driven by the desire to make a better world, stand up for right over wrong, and look after the most vulnerable in society?

It is perfectly possible to combine, as I do, an idealistic belief in healing society, fighting oppression, and looking after the vulnerable – ideals associated with the left – with a more hard-headed commitment to making moral judgments between good and bad behavior, distinguishing between truth and lies and focusing on what is achievable rather than what is desirable only in theory – attributes associated with "the right."

It is surely in this kind of combination that the true "center ground" resides. It is therefore imperative to rescue the language from its left-wing hijackers and restore truth, reason and decency to political debate. Unfortunately, too many conservatives on both sides of the pond have themselves become intimidated, cowed and demoralized by the left's mind-bending discourse. This memoir is an attempt to set the record straight by showing through my personal story what has happened in the West, and thereby suggest how the true center ground can now fight back.

Just as Britain and America did in 2016.

Chapter 1

A PERFECT FAMILY STORM:
THE SHAPING OF A CULTURE WARRIOR

The child lay tensely in the darkness on a bed that was not her own. A crisis had placed her there, an impending and unimaginable horror that only one person could prevent.

That day, her predictable daily routine had been dramatically interrupted. Startled and alarmed, the nine-year-old had been extracted from her classroom and taken by her mother to stay with Pearl, her mother's sister, because her father's youngest sister, Marie, was very ill.

Her mother was distracted, not herself. The child, who had no siblings and who lived inside her mother's skin, was full of dread. This was a family emergency with which her mother would have to deal – because, as everyone knew, she was the only one who could. But the child knew what others did not know, that her mother lived on the edge of a personal precipice from which only the child could prevent her from falling.

Late that night, the child heard the phone shockingly shatter the silence like a sob, and then her aunt's voice rising urgently as she told the person at the other end to "hold on" to herself as Pearl was coming over straightaway. Immediately, the child knew that her mother was at the other end of that call and that her fragile world had fallen apart.

After a day or so had passed, the child returned home. She skipped down the steps to the small flat where she lived. At last she would be reunited with her mother, who would be there as usual with her hugs and tender smile to smooth away all pain and make everything all right again.

But her home was now frighteningly unfamiliar. The front door was swinging open, the hall mirror covered by a white sheet so the child found herself shockingly effaced when she looked at it, and the flat was full of strangers. The child's family was Jewish; after bereavement in observant Jewish households, the close family stay home and are visited by comforters during a week of mourning and prayers called a shiva, when by custom mirrors are covered so that the mourners avoid vanity and concentrate on remembering their loved one.

Disoriented, the child wandered in and was hurried past the closed kitchen door, behind which she could hear someone hysterical and out of control: her mother.

The child had understood enough, from her mother's panic-stricken and terse remarks when she had last seen her, to become frozen in horror. Marie had been taken ill with a life-threatening disease. Her own mother, the child's grandmother, had refused to allow her to be taken to hospital. The child's mother had taken charge of the situation too late. Marie, still in her thirties, had died.

The child understood intuitively that both her parents were consumed by guilt over Marie's death. The child grieved bitterly for both of them. But she knew she dared not utter a word to them about what had happened. She knew instinctively that to do so would send her mother over the edge of that precipice.

From that time onwards, Marie's name was never mentioned again in her hearing by either of her parents. The tragedy hung over the family in a pall of silence. And so the child's universe was permanently darkened by a terrifying shadow, for Marie's death seemed to her to confirm the presence of a monster in her life.

To the child, her grandmother had not only killed Marie but had also reduced another daughter to a kind of zombie and had kept the third in metaphorical chains. And worst of all, she had turned the child's father into a kind of permanent child himself, incapable of doing what a husband and father should do.

In her young mind, her damaged father had failed in turn to protect her mother from this monstrous blight on her life. But worse still, he had also failed in something she would only much later come to realize – providing a crucial escape valve to protect the child from the person she loved more dearly than she could ever love herself.

I was that child. The trauma associated with that family catastrophe has haunted me all my life. But it has taken me a long time fully to understand why those events had such an impact. For behind that tragedy – awful enough in itself as it was – lay a nexus of unhealthy, mind-bending, and destructive family relationships that were indelibly to shape my character and attitudes.

It was to be many years before I came to understand even that there was anything wrong with these suffocating bonds, let alone start to struggle free of them. The ensuing separation involved intense anguish. And it was mirrored and indeed intimately wrapped up with another deeply painful separation, as my political and professional life during more than a quarter of a century became convulsed by developments that led me inexorably to leave my political family behind.

Indeed, just as my real family background shaped what I originally was, finally separating myself from it helped shape what I was to become. And I have felt that traumatic political journey also as a kind of bereavement. My personal and political lives have flowed in and out of each other as if they were tributaries of one great tempestuous river.

I grew up in a family that was typical of the post-Second World War British Jewish community. It was Jewish but not very religious. My parents observed the Jewish dietary rules quite strictly but worked on Saturdays, observing the Sabbath merely through the ritual Friday night meal, and attended synagogue only three times a year on the High Holy Days.

Always self-conscious about being outsiders in British society, they kept their heads down and tried to assimilate by aping the class mannerisms of the English. My father, Alfred, for example, wore a bowler hat, which he perched on his head at an insouciant angle, thus ruining the illusion. After all, he was not a bourgeois or professional but sold women's dresses to shopkeepers from a van; it was my mother, Mabel, who had aspirations to social advancement. That bowler hat was thus always a source of acute embarrassment to me, and perhaps contributed to my lifetime dislike of pretentiousness and social climbing.

They had met in London and married a couple of years after the war. Both came from similar families – working-class and lower-middle-class Jews who had arrived in Britain from Russia and Poland around the turn of the twentieth century – but with one significant difference. My mother was half a social class above my father because her parents, unlike his who had emigrated from Poland, had been born in Britain.

My mother's father was a sign-writer; my father's father, a tailor's cutter. Both my parents were born in London's East End, that collection of impoverished streets that were home to so many immigrant Jews as they are today to fresh generations of incomers.

My mother's family, which moved to slightly more genteel surroundings on the boundary with Essex, was hardly well-off but my father's family was extremely poor. My father's father – who, according to family mythology, was given the name Phillips because the immigration officer couldn't pronounce his Polish name – would stand on the street corner every week in the often unrealized hope of being selected for work.

My father was haunted all his life by the poverty he endured in the East End. He slept four to a room with his sisters; he never had enough to eat. His innate intelligence hit an early cul-de-sac when his parents turned down the grammar school place he had won because they couldn't afford the school uniform, and he left school at the age of thirteen.

Unlike most other Jews from similarly impoverished backgrounds, however, Alfred never prospered enough to do what they eventually managed to do and move into the leafy suburbs. Never understanding the value of property, he died with hardly any savings in the same rented flat in Hammersmith, west London, where he and my mother had lived for half a century. He and Mabel stuck fiercely to the socialist political assumptions that had been an absolute given in their own backgrounds – that there were a boss class and a working class, and that we should never forget (despite my mother's more genteel aspirations) that we belonged to the latter.

Alfred possessed no resources, neither intellectual nor financial: no hinterland of aspiration fulfilled by any subsequent autodidactic determination to fill in the gaps. In truth, he had very little – but he did have me, his only child, of whom he was so poignantly proud. My mother was different. Sensitive and artistic, she had briefly trained as a fashion designer before illness cut that short and she went to work instead in an uncle's shop.

Without question, all this helped shape my fundamental attitudes which remain unchanged to this day. Although my parents were not overly religious in the formal sense, I was brought up on strong Jewish values of family obligation, a fierce sense of right and wrong and the unquestionable assumption that the more fortunate amongst us had an absolute duty to help those who were worse off.

It was Mabel, however, who was the formative influence on my life. I was an only child and there was simply no space at all between my mother and me. We flowed into each other. I adopted her views, her mannerisms, her likes and dislikes. I knew her thoughts before she even thought them, and she mine. I was her passionate partisan.

She was witty, elegant, capable, intelligent, sensitive and beautiful. Other girls had mothers who were too loud, too quiet, too mumsyish, too interfering, too distant, too judgmental. Not mine. In my eyes, she was perfect.

She was the largest thing in my life, the sun that blotted out all other planets. She poured everything she had into me. It was she who decided that, despite the family's modest income, I would be educated at private schools. She made all the decisions about my life.

It was she who gave me a love of books and of reading; she took me to the ballet and the theater. My father was never part of these expeditions. And it was she who mainly imparted those values – an iron sense of duty, a strong belief in fairness, and in standing up for what was right.

But she was emotionally very frail. In 1940, when she was sixteen, she had had a nervous breakdown following her father's death from tuberculosis. Quite why she had been so badly affected, I never discovered: the subject was taboo. But for the rest of her life she suffered psychological problems. There was some baffling sense of guilt, certainly, but that wasn't all. She had a morbid fear of germs and a terror of disease. She would wash her hands, or certain objects such as saucepans, in the same obsessive routines – so many sluices or turns of the tap one way, and then so many in the other. When she locked the front door, the keys had to be turned in a particular rhythm. Then she would rest the flat of her hand on the door and push it a required number of times to make sure it was shut. If she was interrupted in any of these routines, she would have to start all over again. It was all a desperate need to make her world an orderly place under her control, to stop it from disintegrating.

I knew she'd been very ill after I was born. Breast abscesses, I was told. She'd been in hospital with me as a result for a couple of months. It seems a long time for treating abscesses.

It was because she'd been so long in the hospital, my mother told me repeatedly, that she had got into the way of thinking that everything needed to be disinfected all the time, "just like the nurses did." I regarded this as a totally reasonable explanation, just as I never questioned the saucepan-sluicing or the front door-pushing. How could it have been otherwise? My mother was perfect.

But she was also fragile and had to be protected. I was her guardian and her protector. It never even occurred to me that that was properly my father's role. Was he not, after all, just an overgrown child?

I was the focal point of my mother's existence – and, in my mind, the core of her fragility. I knew that because she told me. She was all-powerful, organized, and organizing, and yet I knew that one *snap* of my fingers in her face and I could destroy her.

"No one will ever love you like I do," she would say to me several times a week. "I know that one day you will grow up and leave me and I don't know how I'm going to cope." Of course, I knew from this that when I grew up it would kill her if I left her. I also knew that it would destroy her if I ever made her upset. If I should ever suggest she was not a perfect mother, I would drive her off the edge.

In my childish mind, therefore, I looked after and protected her. I was responsible for her happiness, her sanity and her life. Indeed, had I not been the cause of her frailties simply by being born?

And so I was what is called in the jargon a "parentified child" – in other words, since childhood is all about being looked after free from responsibility, not really a child at all.

The person who should have been the all-important foil to my mother never intruded into the sealed relationship between his wife and his daughter. If only he had been able to do so. If he had, he could have shown me that, far from being perfect, my mother's perspective was so very distorted, and thus he could have freed me, allowing me to feel entitled to live.

Not until many years later did I realize I had never had an independent conversation with my father about anything remotely significant. All such communication was mediated through my mother. It would no more have occurred to me to seek solace, reassurance or enlightenment from him than it would have been to fly to the moon.

The belief that I could never leave her without imperilling her sanity or even her life was deeply to affect my own life as an adult. It was unthinkable, for example, that I could ever have taken a posting as a foreign journalist because I could never have lived abroad. Indeed, for three decades I lived with my husband and children just a few streets away from my parents' flat.

I was in a trap, of course, but that trap also served as my comfort zone. The prospect of leaving it and striking out on my own was terrifying and unthinkable, because it meant facing things I did not want to face. Imprisonment is an affliction, but sometimes its power lies in the fact that it also provides a seductive cocoon. Freedom is often difficult and even painful. In exactly the same way, I was unable to think beyond the confines of the leftism that I could challenge in those early years no more easily than I could have challenged my mother's perfection. And when I did eventually do so, the exhilaration of thinking out of the political box was tempered by the fear and discomfort of doing so.

Of course, I understood none of this while I was growing up. A solitary, serious-minded child who had never known what it really meant to play, I thought my life was happy and normal. I grew up by my mother's side in her shop. For amusement, I would climb inside the large cardboard boxes which had contained deliveries of clothes, close the flaps, and pretend I was hidden from the world; or, I would buy birdseed from the local pet shop and stand for hours in the little park across the road feeding the pigeons, totally absorbed.

Desperate to join in with other children's games, I would hover shyly and nervously at the edge, willing them to ask me to join in. They rarely did. When I was invited to birthday parties I could only goggle in amazement at girls hanging upside down from rope ladders or climbing trees in the garden. I would never have been allowed in case I hurt myself. And I would never do anything that my mother had forbidden.

Never knowing what it was to enjoy the adventure of being alive, I retreated instead into the magical world of books. Words, with which I had a natural fluency, became my allies and the shield behind which I could hide. Working at my schoolbooks made me feel in control. If I worked hard, I could make good things happen.

School was where I felt free and happy – where I had fun. What was fun? The studying. For the child who didn't know how to play, studying was recreation. School became my life, my family. I only had a very small number of friends, but that was enough – that and the broader community of girls and teachers, the whole collective life of the school of which I felt so intensely a part.

Not that I was ever quite like the other girls at Putney High School in southwest London. From adolescence onwards, parties with boys from local schools became a feature of weekend life – for the others. My mother forbade me from going to them, as there was apparently an unbroken line from such pursuits to marrying outside the Jewish people, which I knew would kill both my parents. When I was allowed to attend rare all-girl social occasions, I was open-mouthed at the sophisticated, sexy clothes the others wore because, out of school, I still dressed like a schoolgirl.

None of these differences or restrictions I ever thought odd or oppressive. I never rebelled, never stayed out late at night or went off secretly to a rock concert or spent my pocket money on furry false eyelashes or read mildly lubricious romantic magazines. My mother laid down the rules and I never questioned any of them. How could I have done otherwise? I knew that if I ever caused her to think she wasn't a perfect mother it would destroy her. And, of course, she was my perfect, adored, idolized mother. But without acknowledging the sharp contradiction, I always harbored a secret fantasy that I was actually an adopted child.

Why, though, was my father incapable of acting as the crucial foil to my mother? The reason was that he too was crippled by his own background – by his mother who, to my childish eyes at least, had caused the death of one of his own sisters.

When I was tiny, my father's mother lived in a grim slum in Islington, north London, in a house owned by a rapacious landlord. The street was called Duncan Terrace. Today, a house there sells for upwards of £2 million. It is a fine Georgian terrace with beautiful oval windows on the ground floor. I suppose the shape of those windows must have imprinted themselves on my infant mind as representing something quite terrifying. To this day I cannot look at upright oval shapes – the stained glass windows of a cathedral, for example, or the "Golden Arches" of McDonalds, or even a lowercase letter "m" – without my heart lurching, absurdly, into my mouth.

In later years, when we visited this grandmother every other Sunday afternoon, I used to wait for the moment when we left and the front door closed behind us. Finally I felt I could breathe. For that precious single instant, I was free. Maybe, I felt, I could hold that moment forever. But, of course, no sooner had it arrived than it vanished, and so the inexorable countdown started once again.

For it was only at that single, perfect moment when the door closed behind me that it was a full two weeks before I would have to visit that grandmother again. Every moment that subsequently passed would bring the fortnightly ordeal nearer.

But what could have caused such a blight on a small child's life, such shrinking dread? Who other than those who enter the world of a child may properly appreciate the incontrovertible logic by which intuited fury and incipient hysteria can settle in a childish universe into the shape of a monster unleashing untold terrors? A monster who threatens to smash that child's world into fragments by seeming to drive the two people who formed it apart? Booba, we called her, my cousins and I – Yiddish for grandmother. Her first language was the Yiddish she had spoken in the close-knit Jewish community of her native Poland. Even today, when I hear someone called "Booba" I recoil, and yet I observe to my astonishment that whoever it is appears to be a perfectly normal, pleasant woman.

Now that I am myself a grandmother – but not, most definitely not, "Booba" – playing with my own grandchildren, reading to them, listening to their chatter, and cuddling them as they leap into my lap, I can see how odd was my own situation as a child. I don't think I ever voluntarily approached or touched Booba. As far as I recall, she never hugged me, played with me, nor indeed said anything to me at all. Did she want to? I will never know. What stopped her? That, I think, I do know.

Booba was a heavy woman with a thin mouth. She looked like the Polish farm girl she once had been. She habitually wore a wraparound floral apron and carpet slippers shaped like boots. When she laughed, I saw a cackling crone: Booba possessed alarmingly few teeth because she was too frightened to go the dentist, but not as determined as she was never to go near a hospital where she believed you would almost certainly be killed.

The flat where she lived in later years was in a council block in Swiss Cottage, northwest London, six floors up stone stairs on which the fumes of disinfectant barely masked other more distasteful smells and which we had to navigate because my father, who was terrified of enclosed spaces, refused ever to use a lift.

The television in the flat was always on, showing old films starring Bette Davis, Clark Gable, or Joan Crawford. When we arrived, my mother would ask pointedly for the sound to be turned down. I knew that having the TV on in the middle of the day was a sign of moral weakness. It was never on during the day at home apart from the annual FA Cup Final, when my father tore himself away from the children's clothes shop my mother ran and where he would make himself a weekly nuisance on a Saturday; or when I was allowed to watch children's TV on a Thursday afternoon, the shop's early closing day and the one precious afternoon therefore when I went straight home from school.

And yet at Booba's I would sit crouched on a chair up against the TV, my ear so close to the set I could scarcely focus on the picture. If I could have melted through the cathode-ray tube into the movie I would gladly have done so. I could not endure what I was picking up in the room, as if I were a human antenna into which were being channelled signals of distress. It was imperative to drown out the sound of my father's voice railing plaintively and impotently against his mother, and my own mother's anger undetected by all but myself.

By the time I got home, I would already have been forced to listen to the inevitable row, the bitter recriminations and dumb misery which tore me in two. And with every day that passed, the dread of the next visit would spread like a fog around my heart.

What were they arguing about? The specifics were always far too banal and trivial to be recollected. But the real issue underlying them all was as momentous as they come. It was that Booba would require my father to dance attendance upon her and turn his life inside out in order to place her, rather than his wife and daughter, at its center while she made herself as uncooperative as it was possible to be.

He visited her twice a week, Mondays and Wednesdays, in addition to our fortnightly family appearance. He couldn't do enough for her; indeed, it was never enough, and my mother usually ended up doing it anyway because, as everyone knew, she was so very capable.

My father might shout at Booba, but he always, always gave in. How desperately I wanted him to stand his ground, give her an ultimatum, turn his back upon such unnatural bullying and at last put his wife, my mother rather than his own, first in his life. But he never did. The more he shouted and revealed his own inadequacy, the more my infant self writhed, recoiled, and raged. The bitter recriminations that my mother hurled at my father as we travelled back home from our visits, with my father behaving like a cornered animal, made me feel as if my whole universe was about to disintegrate.

Maybe my impression of Booba was unfair, in which case I am truly sorry. As an ignorant and illiterate Polish Jewish immigrant, sent to Britain as a young girl at the turn of the twentieth century by an apparently unloving family that, for unexplained reasons, wanted to get rid of her, she had had a hard life. But to me as a child she was the most terrifying figure possible – a destroyer of her children.

In addition to my father, Booba had three daughters. Two of them, Betty and Marie, lived with her until death parted them. When we visited, they were always there. These two unfortunates appeared to have virtually no life whatsoever beyond their mother's baleful presence.

For reasons no one ever explained to me and I was too afraid to solicit, Marie's chin rested permanently on her chest. To me, this poor, crippled girl seemed to have stepped out of one of the dark and menacing folktales I consumed from the local library.

Betty, who walked with a limp resulting from botched surgery after a factory accident, seemed to be herself a child in a broken adult body. On my visits she would baffle me by urging me to admire her latest acquisition, some tawdry piece of plastic jewelry from Woolworth's or the like, which she would hold out to be shown off, as does a five-year-old, with undiscriminating pride.

No one ever explained to me that Betty suffered what would nowadays probably would be called a "learning disability." Occasionally my mother would murmur that she was "simple," but bewilderingly everyone else seemed to treat her as a perfectly competent adult just given to doing extremely stupid things that exasperated them – and caused them to shout at her as if she were capable of rational response.

To everyone's astonishment and no small consternation, in late middle age she married an elderly male pen-pal friend who seemed almost as "simple" as she was. Unsurprisingly, he also moved in with Booba.

Later, after both her mother and husband had died, Betty would occasionally set fire to her flat when she was lighting candles to inaugurate the Sabbath. My father would hang up the phone after an urgent call about her latest calamity and put his head in his hands. I wept both for him and for the sister over whom he was always in such impotent anguish.

The person with whom he would have these painful phone conversations was his other sister, Sally, who lived next door to Booba and her ménage. Ostensibly Sally, her husband, and their two sons lived an independent life – but in reality, Sally was bound to her mother and her controlling demands with hoops of steel.

The walls between the two flats seemed entirely permeable; not only were Sally and family constantly shuttling next door, but these lives seemed inextricably welded together. And this permeability seemed to extend to the little flat in Hammersmith where my parents and I lived.

Virtually every cough, sneeze, stomachache, headache, earache, ingrown toenail, or bout of indigestion experienced in Swiss Cottage was conveyed to my father. He would then report all this in doom-laden tones, plus Booba's latest demands, to my mother, who would smolder with the suppressed fury that so frightened me – and who would then dispense advice and suggestions to smooth away all the problems, which would be conveyed back to Swiss Cottage.

My mother, Mabel, was the problem-solver. She was governed by one overriding imperative – to keep the family peace. She would rage at my father, but then she would swallow her fury and do whatever was required to prevent her greatest dread, a *broiges* or family feud. Her terror that anger might drive any of us apart appeared to derive from the pathological guilt she suffered. If someone else in the family – her entire world – behaved badly, she simply couldn't cope with the guilt she would inescapably feel if this resulted in division. And so she would put aside her own wishes and do whatever was necessary to pacify her mother-in-law, avoid family feuds at all costs, and make my father content.

From infancy onwards, I would observe all this and silently grieve. It was all so horribly unfair. Bad deeds were not just going unpunished but were even being rewarded. My mother was being martyred and my father was allowing this to happen. He himself was being bullied and was weakly giving in. Why couldn't he be a proper grown-up and look after my mother instead of having her run after his family?

The answer was that my father was also consumed by guilt. He felt that by marrying Mabel and living a few miles away from his family he had escaped, and so he had to do his bit. But to me he had not escaped at all. To me he had been turned into a shadow of a husband and a nonexistent father. He seemed incapable of autonomous action. Physically present in my daily life, as my other parent he just wasn't there.

In fact, to my childish eyes, fathers throughout my family just "weren't there." Not that anyone was divorced or a single parent as they are today – my family was a solidly nuclear, traditional sort. But the fathers tended to be bossed around as if they were children and treated like imbeciles – if they even existed at all.

My mother's father had died well before I was born. My father's father died when I was a tiny child. I believe they were both meek, gentle men. Both my grandmothers were strong women who laid down the law. My maternal grandmother was often referred to admiringly by other members of the family as "the matriarch." Various uncles appeared to be generally squashed by their wives from whom they retreated for a quiet life. And my own father – well, unfortunately he seemed to me to be just a shell. Treated by his mother as if he owed her the duties of a husband, and by his wife as if he were a helpless infant, he simply didn't figure in my childish universe other than as a benign but entirely passive presence.

I loved my father very much – he was gentle, kind, and innocent. And he had a great sense of humor. I always looked forward to hearing what had happened to him during his working day, stories he unloaded every evening upon my mother and me, which generally featured scheming bosses who lived in expensive houses, the gossipy customers for the ladies' clothing he sold from a van, the Nazi-style traffic wardens. But his apparent powerlessness and the way he seemed always to be trampled upon upset me very badly. It gave me a lifelong passion to stand up for the vulnerable – and it also provided me with the insight that sometimes the vulnerable can be ill-served by those who appear closest to them.

I don't remember my father's father, my *zaida*, at all, even though I was four years old when he died. What I do remember is my father's reaction to his death, as I peeped from the doorway to see him sitting at the dining table with a glass of whisky, crying. I realized something truly terrible had happened. I had never seen my father drink whisky during the day before, and I had certainly never seen him cry. But I wasn't allowed to go to him. My mother's reaction to grief, as it was to rage, was to pretend it didn't exist.

I was not allowed to see anyone being "upset." When we visited a house where a family was sitting *shiva* – the seven days of mourning observed in traditional Jewish households for a relative who has died – I was invariably left in the car, supplied with sandwiches and books, for the hour or so my parents were inside. It was the same with death itself. No one ever died. They simply vanished. "Very sad news," my mother would announce, "about Great-Uncle or Great-Auntie So-and-So." And she would shake her head sorrowfully. What the sad news was, she never said; but of course I knew. And I also knew that death and distress were to be erased from existence.

When I was about twelve years old, my mother developed what she described as tingling in her legs and "funny feelings" when she walked too far. She consulted an eminent neurologist whom she saw for the next quarter of a century, during which time she described her nameless and strange affliction as "my condition," which is how the neurologist had described it to her. Neither my father nor I ever thought of questioning this meaningless diagnosis.

When I went to university, she visibly steeled herself against my departure. I knew it was a crisis. I was leaving her bereft. I couldn't do that. And so I slipped into a pattern of seeing her every two weeks; either I would go home or my parents would come to Oxford. And of course, I would call her several times a week too. Physically in Oxford, I mentally never left home. At best it felt as if I was on the end of a long leash. I was there on license.

Oxford, where I read English Literature at St Anne's college, passed as in a dream. On the last day of finals, everyone else flung off their academic dress and set about having a great time enjoying student life in that beautiful city, punting on the river and partying, finally free of the demands of studying. But as soon as I finished my last exam, I went straight back to London still in my black-and-white academic uniform, straight to my mother's shop. It was as if I was saying to her, look, you see, I didn't really leave you after all.

But, to my dismay, she did not greet me as I had imagined. She was vacant, detached, barely registering that I was there. She was already sinking into the depression which a few months later would result one night in my father shouting in panic for me to wake up: I was by now enrolled in a journalism training course in Cardiff, but still coming home every two weeks. Emerging from my room, I found my mother sitting at the kitchen table as if in a trance, totally immobile and not saying a word. That was the day a psychiatrist arrived and gave her the first of a series of injections, after which she returned to us, still very distant but at least responding to us and no longer immobile. And yet even during my mother's whole terrifying collapse, still my father never had a proper conversation with me about her or anything personal, nor did I ever attempt to speak to him. It would have felt like disloyalty.

At Oxford, finally presented with freedom, I still never slipped the leash. I even arrived as an undergraduate with a mother-approved boyfriend from London in tow. Joshua was in his final year studying law when I began reading for my English degree, but I had been going out with him since I was sixteen.

Joshua was clever, quirky, a dazzlingly witty debater. He was given to bursts of extravagant zaniness – in order to try out his legal expertise he once sued the laundry in Oxford for losing a treasured shirt; on another occasion he hitchhiked from Stockholm to Genoa in order to surprise me on my mother-approved first-ever trip abroad without my parents (I was then eighteen.) But what really hooked me to Joshua – for life, as it turned out – was that he made me laugh. He was fun to be with.

At Oxford I dabbled in student politics in mildly left-wing circles. I joined in the self-important protests against the low wages and poor working conditions for the college cleaners, and waved placards on demonstrations against the then-education minister, one Margaret Thatcher. I grew my hair into a hippie-ish thicket and sloped around affecting a worldly swagger – while inside I was privately shrinking. I was too shy to make more than a tiny number of friends, to whom I subsequently clung, and was permanently intimidated both by my tutors and socially confident fellow students.

Years later, however, I was told that at the time I myself had given an impression of supreme (and supremely irritating) confidence by holding forth in college. Indeed, I was even elected president of its student body, the junior common room. So how did I manage to give an impression that was so totally at odds with what I actually felt? I believe it was a combination of two things: my facility with words, and a compulsion to place myself at the center of the stage in order to validate my existence by the approval of an audience.

So it would appear that journalism and I were ideally suited to each other. What else, after all, drives journalism? Why else would journalists voluntarily put themselves through the daily agonies of writing to nail-biting deadlines, clawing their way over rapacious colleagues, and exposing themselves to the risk of criticism, ridicule, or worse by placing what they write before the public, if not from a compulsion (often doomed) to attract the applause of an audience?

Not that a life in journalism had always beckoned. At Oxford, after receiving an early and demoralizing rebuff, I disdained student journalism altogether as being peopled by unprincipled careerist creeps. Not knowing what I wanted to do in life, I sent off applications for a variety of different careers

– and, despite my contempt for student journalism, sent an application just for the hell of it to a newspaper training group.

To my astonishment and no small dismay, this offered me a two-year training post on the Hemel Hempstead *Evening Echo*, which served a commuter town just north of London. Dismay, because I realized I would have to do what I flinched from doing: put myself about, talk to total strangers, somehow wheedle out of them information they would not want to give me.

But of course, I couldn't turn such a glittering opportunity down. So I found myself on the *Echo*, newly married to Joshua, being sent out in misery to interview the newly bereaved in order to extract a photograph from them of their deceased loved one, enduring the numbing tedium of local council meetings, writing up court cases of extreme banality ("get the ****ing sex in the headline!" I was told), crashing the office cars (I had only recently passed my driving test by the skin of my teeth), and being shouted at by the archetypal news editor who thought university ***ing graduates were ridiculously up themselves and a total pain in the backside.

It was great training. I couldn't get away from there fast enough. With no national newspaper prepared to take me on, however, I gratefully took a post on *New Society* magazine, a well-respected weekly periodical devoted to worthy articles about social policy. It was a useful steppingstone.

Chapter 2

THE GUARDIAN OF EDEN:
I ARRIVE IN PARADISE

In 1977, at the age of twenty-six, I joined the staff of *The Guardian*. The very way I was hired was itself a telling foretaste of the convolutions in store. I had been writing for a year for *New Society*. While there, I was named Young Journalist of the Year in the annual press awards for my earlier work on the *Evening Echo*, which brought me to wider attention. Having applied for a reporter's job at *The Guardian*, I was wildly excited to be invited for an interview with the editor, Peter Preston. A Fleet Street newspaper! I was dazzled. Not that it was actually in Fleet Street, the legendary home of national newspapers; *The Guardian* was housed in a squat, featureless building in Clerkenwell, a short distance away. Never mind: *The Guardian* was one of Britain's most distinguished and influential national newspapers, the paper of choice for intellectuals, the voice of progressive conscience and the dream destination for many, if not most, aspiring journalists.

I prepared assiduously for the encounter. I rehearsed answers to likely questions such as why I wanted to be a reporter, why for *The Guardian*, what my interests were, my political views, how I saw my career developing.

I was asked none of these things. Instead Preston, looking for the most part not at me but at a place on the wall behind me, started by apologizing that he could not offer me a specialist reporter's job and mumbled something unintelligible about being in touch with the details. That was it. At no point was I ever offered, in terms, a job at *The Guardian*. As in so many encounters at the paper, one was left to intuit as if by osmosis through a murk of significant silences and conveniently deniable obfuscation.

I joined the paper as a general reporter but, given my previous experience in writing about social issues, soon found myself promoted to be the paper's social services correspondent. In those early years, I was thrilled to be a *Guardian* reporter. It was all wonderfully casual, young and fun. Reporters slopped around in jeans and scruffy jackets. I thought that was delightful. The filing cabinets were bright red. I thought that was delightful. The newsroom had the atmosphere of an Oxford junior common room. I thought that was particularly delightful. Joshua and I had moved to west London mainly so that I could be near my parents. Finally, I could enjoy a university atmosphere without any guilt.

In those early years I was treated, most flatteringly, as a talent that had to be carefully nurtured to fulfill some perceived future promise. I felt looked after in particular by two or three senior colleagues who kindly took it upon themselves to act as mentors. I felt loved and cherished. It was as if I were the favored child of a wonderful and impressive family.

One day a new reporter arrived. He looked a bit lost and lonely and so I felt sorry for him. I knew just how he felt. I invited him to come and sit at a spare desk next to me and my affable colleague Richard Norton-Taylor. His name was Alan Rusbridger. He turned out to be highly gifted, creative, and musical. His talents seemed to me to be wasted in the newsroom. Taking a kindly interest in his welfare, I suggested that he had it in him to become instead a clever and witty playwright – another Michael Frayn, perhaps. Modestly, he demurred. I thought he was just too diffident ever to achieve what he was clearly capable of doing.

This was an early sign of my less-than-stellar talent at office politics – my naive tendency to take people at face value and fail to perceive the blade inside the velvet glove. Alan would eventually become editor of *The Guardian*, displaying a ruthless ambition even greater than his charm, at around the very time that my own increasingly unhappy tenure at *The Guardian* newspaper was drawing to its traumatic close.

The Guardian, during the period I was there, was distinguished by two notable characteristics: the endless whining and conspiratorial bent of its staff, and their devotion and loyalty to a paper about which they never ceased complaining. What did they whine about? Well, pretty well everything. They whined about the way their copy was treated by the sub-editors, about the editorial priorities of the front-page news stories, about the editorial priorities of the inside-page news stories, about any changes to the office furniture or seating arrangements, about the introduction of hideously alien computers (when I joined the staff, copy was typed on typewriters).

And there were always plots, and dark suspicions about plots, over who was likely to be promoted or moved sideways, over what the presence of this person or that in the editor's office might signify (traffic into his room was assiduously monitored), or the sinister hidden meaning beneath the latest opaque stream of consciousness from Peter Preston. To some extent, the whining and the plotting resulted from a radical insecurity among the journalists caused by Preston's much-resented approach to staff management – the ironically named "creative tension" – which the journalists hated because they felt they were being measured against each other.

But the whining and the plotting were surely in the main a byproduct of the defining feature of *Guardian* journalists – a narcissistic self-regard based upon a fixed belief in their own superiority and righteousness, nurtured by indulgence and privilege.

We believed that *The Guardian* was simply more civilized than any other newspaper in Britain. Indeed, "civilized" was the word frequently on our lips as we congratulated ourselves for being quite different from the rapacious and unprincipled rogues, spivs, and thugs employed in the rest of Fleet Street. Unlike them, we had no nasty, evil proprietor telling us what line to take. Unlike them, we never ever paid any money for stories, thus compromising the integrity of the information our sources provided. Unlike them, we never descended to the vulgar cesspools of personality or celebrity-driven tittle-tattle. Ugh!

We were, by contrast, the sea-green incorruptibles, high-minded to a fault, not owned by any plutocrat with a power mania but run instead by a trust whose sole purpose was to keep *The Guardian* going in perpetuity in order to continue publishing its elevated journalism. We were the only truly independent paper on which no one told any writer what to write (when *The Independent* newspaper opened in 1986, *The Guardian* was beside itself in dismay, indignation, and fury).

We were above all a writers' newspaper, where words were treated with reverence and fine writing was much lionized and encouraged. This remains as true today as it was then. It was not just opinion pieces or feature articles that were carefully crafted, elegant pieces of prose, but the news stories, cricket, and football commentaries and of course the theater and book reviews. It all radiated education, intelligence, and wit.

In 1977, the paper published a seven-page supplement about the island of San Serriffe, with advertisements from major companies congratulating the country on the tenth anniversary of its independence. Many readers hardly glanced at the pages of worthy reports on the island's topography, politics, culture, and so on – such sponsored supplements were common at the time – and so failed to notice that the whole thing was a glorious April 1 spoof. "Sans serif" is a typographical term, and the elaborate description of the fictional island – supposedly shaped like a semi-colon – was studded with typographical and printers' puns. It fooled many and passed into folklore: an extended joke that actually made money. How proud we all were to work for such a clever, amusing, and brilliant paper!

We also admired what we told ourselves was the paper's historically noble and principled stand in defense of liberty and justice and against oppression. We were proud of its nonconformist origins as the *Manchester Guardian* and proud of its legendary former editor CP Scott who coined the dictum, "comment is free but facts are sacred." It was only later that I realized there was more than a shred of truth in the old joke that *Guardian* news stories freely spun the facts while its editorial comment columns treated opinion as sacred.

No one ever mentioned the paper's unfortunate support in the 1930s for Stalinism, when it sacked its Moscow correspondent Malcolm Muggeridge after he had tried to report the effects of the bureaucrat-induced famine in the Ukraine and Caucasus in which some six million people starved to death. To us, however, Malcolm Muggeridge – who in his later years became a Catholic moral campaigner – was in his old age merely a synonym for the kind of closed-minded, right-wing reactionary who inveighed against sex and violence in British society.

For progressives like us, such people did not evoke merely an intellectual disdain. There was also a strong element of aesthetic distaste. People on the right seemed unattractively crabby and sour. People on the left had an altogether more generous view of human nature and the world. Whereas the right seemed to believe the worst of people, we believed the best. They embodied darkness; we embodied light. They were about the past; we were always looking to the future. They stood for feathering their own nests and defending the indefensible status quo. We stood for fairness and equality, for protecting the weak and vulnerable, for standing against tyranny and prejudice.

We were the embodiment of virtue itself. Everybody who was not one of us automatically placed themselves beyond the moral pale, on the other side from all that was good and decent and just. Whatever we said was, by definition, morally correct.

Whatever they said could therefore be safely discounted. Everyone who was not one of us was the opposite of us. We were the left; therefore, everyone who was not the left was the right. The right was evil; everyone not on the left was therefore evil. The word "Manichaean" was not at that time part of my vocabulary.

Not that I actually regarded myself as a left-winger. I always thought of myself as a liberal, in the classical, English meaning of the word, which to me was another way of saying I believed in progress and the capacity of human beings to create a better world. But that was fine – I was a perfect fit at *The Guardian* because I thought it was a liberal paper, as indeed it really had been when it was the *Manchester Guardian*. "Liberal" and "left-wing" were the same thing, I assumed, as they were both used interchangeably with "progressive." Indeed, in Britain the left refers to itself constantly as the "liberal left." Only much later did I realize that the left is fundamentally illiberal.

As the center of moral gravity, the "liberal left" therefore also constituted the political "center ground." That meant that everything not on the left was politically extreme. A glancing reference in *The Guardian* in 2012 illustrated how this appropriation of the center ground had become axiomatic. Referring to the fact that the sun had shone on a *Guardian* access weekend, Stephen Moss quipped "God is a centrist" (*The Guardian*, March 26, 2012).

It is hard to exaggerate the importance of this utterly false axiom. For by asserting that it embodied the center ground, what the left actually did was to hijack the center ground and substitute its own extreme values – thus shifting Britain's center of political and moral gravity to the left and besmirching as extremists those on the true center ground. Something very similar has also happened in the US, where language has been appropriated in order to engineer a seismic shift in attitudes concealed by a mind-bending reversal of the meaning of words.

The story of my trajectory at *The Guardian* is also the story of how I only slowly realized both the Orwellian nature and shattering significance of what had happened to Britain and the rest of the Western world. But in those early years, when I too was one of the elect, I shared the delusion. If I had been a character in one of the Mister Men books, I would surely have been Little Miss Guardianista.

On these issues, the left has not changed one iota. What changed was me, as the scales gradually fell from my eyes. But if the left is bewildered by my subsequent self-imposed exile from Eden, those who are not on the left are equally perplexed that I could ever have subscribed to such stupidity, hypocrisy and moral blindness. To which I can only say, by way of explanation, that it was tribal.

I came from the kind of family in which it was simply unthinkable for anyone to have voted Conservative. Voting anything other than Labour would have been seen as a class betrayal. For my parents, it was very simple. The Conservative party represented the boss class, while Labour represented the little man – people like us. Until 1977, my father read the down-market *Daily Express*. Actually, he read only the sports pages at the back; the rest of it, he said, was "rubbish."

When I joined *The Guardian*, however, he started to buy that – and to my astonishment became a most enthusiastic fan. Not only did he exult in the luminous nature of its sports reporting, but he delighted in the quality of writing throughout the paper. Touched by his loyalty, I observed in wonderment how he now devoured its news and opinion pages and would hold forth with animation on its reports and political views. I felt almost as if he had somehow got to university after all. And so my bond with the paper, which was now bringing such benefit not just to me, who had everything, but to my father, who had nothing, was cemented still further.

Chapter 3

LITTLE MISS GUARDIANISTA:
THE DARLING OF THE LEFT

In the late 1970s and early 1980s, at the end of James Callaghan's Labour government and the very beginning of Margaret Thatcher's period in power, I generally toed the standard leftist line.

That agenda was a set of dogmatic mantras. Poverty was bad, cuts in public spending were bad, prison was bad, the Tory government was bad, the state was good, poor people were good, minorities were good, sexual freedom was good. During this period, British society underwent the equivalent of a cultural revolution. People talk of the "swinging sixties" as the decade when the West was swept along by the sexual revolution and insurrectionary student agitation. But it was during the seventies and eighties when those ideas actually became embedded in British society, when the students and young agitators of the sixties became lawyers, teachers, university lecturers, civil servants, campaigners, think-tankers, and politicians – and thus captured the citadels of British culture, where they proceeded to undermine core values of education, family, law, and other cultural building blocks of society.

Yet of all this revolutionary ferment there was little sign in my own writing during those early years at *The Guardian*. There was virtually no questioning of the iron assumption that the poor and socially disadvantaged were inevitably the victims of circumstances rather than accountable for their own behavior, or that the state was a wholly benign actor in the lives of individuals, or that the clean-up TV campaigner Mary Whitehouse was utterly "out-to-lunch." How could there have been? It never occurred to me that there could seriously be another way of looking at the world. If I had doubts, it must mean there was something wrong with me. My colleagues all thought in a similar way; so did my friends and family.

And we all knew one thing above all else – that we were on the side of the angels, and across the barricades hatchet-faced right-wingers represented the dark forces of human nature and society that we were all so proud to be against. With what grim joy we watched the blue-rinse brigade at the annual Conservative party conference baying for the return of corporal punishment and the death penalty. Yes, we shuddered to each other, yes there it was, the proof that the Conservatives really were a breed apart. Of course, we were different; we were of superior morality and intellect. We needed the Conservatives to be stupid and cruel. We defined ourselves by what we were not.

Despite my tribal liberal-leftism, there were, nevertheless, early on, some tiny signs of dangerously independent thought. On one occasion, while writing for *New Society*, I displayed some disdain for the free pass that minorities were afforded by victim culture. After talking to residents of Brixton in 1976 about the local crime rate, I wrote: "Delinquency among young

West Indians is causing concern…[This] alienation cannot be blamed entirely on white society. Some of it seems to stem from their own family background."

In 1978, I wrote an unsigned leading article for *New Society* in the wake of yet another scandal of cruelty and neglect at a psychiatric hospital. I argued that this provided ammunition for those who wanted to bulldoze such hospitals and house their inmates in the community instead, an idea I described as "pie in the sky." I wrote: "There will always be people whose handicaps are so severe they need to be in a hospital." Such places should not be grim fortresses, I accepted, but any chance of improving them was being destroyed by the "strident, fashionable and unrealistic campaign for community care" (*New Society*, November 30, 1978).

This piece provoked some outrage. It was the first time I had come up against the defining stance of the left – that only one view was to be permitted, with no deviations. I was startled, but what had prompted me into challenging this shibboleth was that, as a cub reporter in Hemel Hempstead, I had written about a number of these institutions of which there happened to be several in the area. I had seen for myself that, along with their potential for abuse, they filled a role that simply could not be replicated in the wider community.

Now, though, for the first time I saw how the pursuit by the left of an abstract ideal risked abandoning the vulnerable – and that the left just didn't care. The abstract ideal, that all such patients should live "normally" just like other people, was simply so important that evidence and experience counted for nothing. But I was not driven by ideology. I simply went where the evidence led me. And in time, this would lead me into head-on confrontation with the left, who had replaced truth with ideology and whose weapon of choice against all dissent was vilification and demonization.

As *The Guardian* social services correspondent, I raised eyebrows by taking a critical attitude towards the social work profession. Most specialist reporters avoid antagonizing the people about whom they write because it is from them that such journalists get stories. If you put their backs up, those sources will dry up. Journalists thus become complicit in what can amount to a conspiracy by professional elites against ordinary people. I refused to do that. I always saw my role as telling truth to power, and from my earliest time in journalism I concluded that professional, academic elites had to be robustly interrogated in order to serve the interests of the public. This was an approach which, a few years down the line, was to bring me into serious conflict with both colleagues and the wider middle-class establishment, just as going where the evidence led me would similarly cause me endless trouble.

And below the radar my own views were subtly beginning to shift. Margaret Thatcher had come to power in 1979, and although at *The Guardian* it was an unchallengeable given that she was a heartless, narrow-minded, suburban nightmare I was listening, despite myself, to a point of view I had not heard before.

These Thatcherites were not the usual Conservative upperclass squires; ironically, those toffs tended to be the "wets," or more liberal Tories. The Thatcherites mainly came from the lower or middle-middle class. They were people whose backgrounds were similar to my own. They were promoting the values with which I had been brought up – Labour-supporting family that mine was – all about opportunities for social betterment, hard work, taking responsibility for oneself. And since I never was a Marxist true believer, more a mere cultural lefty for whom a dialectic was possibly something to do with a telephone or else a remedy for kidney disease, I looked at the Thatcher government and wondered whether what I was hearing was at the very least a case that, in all fairness, required an answer.

I had never previously challenged the assumption that the primary duty of the state was to alleviate poverty. My father's still-shuddering memories of not having had enough to eat as a child, and his fierce hatred of those who he thought now intended to "bring back the workhouse," cut very deep. But the early certainties of my *New Society* days were being challenged by trudging round the houses of the poor on godforsaken estates and seeing something way beyond physical need.

What I saw was a spiritual poverty that could not be explained away by material deprivation. Some, for example old people, were truly very poor, unable to heat their houses as well as feed themselves. But in other houses I encountered squalor, filth, and gross neglect but also video recorders, freezers, expensive bikes for the kids. This started to gnaw away at me. How could such people be poor if they had these things? Moreover, a number of them were clearly cheating or could have obtained a job for low pay. It seemed to me that some of the poor were indeed "deserving" while others were not. But that went straight back to the Poor Law, Dickens, the workhouse! How could I possibly think such a heartless thing?

I sought answers. I sat in seminars of grindingly earnest tedium listening to arguments about "relative poverty," which apparently meant that even if people had refrigerator-freezers and video-recorders they were still poor as long as they didn't have all the things others had. This worried me even more. Since the consumer society meant people were getting more and more stuff all the time, it surely followed that poverty would be institutionalized as a permanent feature of society from which there was never to be any escape.

As I pondered all this, I kept such heretical thoughts to myself. Instinctively, I knew that there could be no discussion about them that would not immediately bring down accusations of treachery upon my head. A few years later, I mentioned such thinking to one of my mentors. I felt safe enough with him to raise the dilemma I perceived – that income equality was intrinsically unattainable and a recipe for permanently institutionalized poverty. "Well, that's no reason not to try to achieve it," he snapped, and stalked off.

I felt as if I had been slapped in the face. He was such a thoughtful person, independent-minded, intellectually curious – or so I had always thought. Why then had he behaved as if I were a person he would find it offensive even to talk to, all because I had asked a question?

To try to expunge the feeling that I had been somehow branded, I expressed to another colleague the tentative view that poor people had once seemed to possess more self-reliance and ability to cope with disadvantage than was now apparent, with all the relative beneficence of the welfare state.

"Ah," he drawled, "but then you had the Torah."

If I fondly imagined that I was just one of *The Guardian* gang, the same as everyone else, I couldn't have been more wrong.

I had never thought of myself as a "Jewish writer;" at that stage, with a brief to cover British social issues, I hardly ever wrote about specifically Jewish topics. In fact, the Jewish values I had absorbed from my family background informed everything I thought. There was my fundamental commitment to "heal the world," which is a defining Jewish ethic (although strictly speaking it is the province of the Almighty rather than mankind); there was also my no less fundamental attachment to reason, truth, and logical argument, all of which have deep roots in the Hebrew Bible and in Talmudic exegesis.

Indeed, maybe I would never have been the contrarian I became had I not belonged to a people considered the most argumentative in the world. What I failed to realize at the time, however, was that these characteristics were increasingly setting me apart from those who were going along with the great secular onslaught on the Judeo-Christian roots of the West. While I may not have thought twice about the fact that I was a Jew, they would come to look at me through very different eyes.

Chapter 4

A DEFINING MOMENT:
THE IRON ENTERS MY SOUL

All this was by way of a sideshow compared to what was about to take place while I was a leader-writer for the paper.

I joined the team writing the paper's editorials, or leaders, at the end of 1980. Fortune seemed to be smiling on me. I had just won a national press award for my reporting, specifically for revealing that immigrant Asian women were being given virginity tests at Heathrow airport in an attempt to discover whether they were breaching immigration rules about their married status. The policy ended on the day my story led the front page.

The timing of my award could not have been more auspicious. Early in 1980, when I realized I was pregnant, I decided I wanted to work part-time, at least while the baby was very small. When I plucked up courage to ask for this concession Peter Preston, who was fearful of setting a precedent for his female staff, broke the news of my award to me and observed with a rueful smile that I had him cornered. He suggested I join the leader-writing team part-time, and I jumped at the chance.

When my son Gabriel was born, I took four months' leave. This was a traumatic period. Motherhood hit me like a wrecking ball. I felt trapped and wretched – and deeply ashamed, because I considered this to be an unforgivable response to the great gift of a healthy, beautiful baby. So I told no one and sought no help. My mother was on the scene every day, "just popping in" during her lunch hour at the nearby office where she now worked. I longed for her to arrive – but as soon as she did, far from feeling relief I was unaccountably angry and longed for her to go. What was wrong with me?

Now, in retrospect, it is all too obvious. Inadequately mothered because I had never been allowed to be a child, I found being a mother myself extremely difficult. And now, far from making everything better as she once had done, my mother's very presence – which inevitably required me yet again to "mother her" – could only provoke an incoherent anger and further depression.

I pushed all this to the back of my mind. I also pushed aside the fact that she seemed to be finding it more and more exhausting to walk.

In due course, the cavalry arrived in the form of Frances, a children's nanny of great competence who was to work for us for some five years. I returned to work part-time, embarking on the daily maternal guilt-trip and juggling the irreconcilable pressures of work and children which even a splendid nanny could not alleviate.

At work, at least, I was happy. The leader team represented *The Guardian* at its most collegiate. As a group, its members resembled not so much a newsroom as a university seminar. The leaders were generally thoughtful, balanced and scholarly. I wrote the ones about social policy and I loved writing them. It was all so…well, civilized. Preston allowed his leader-writers a long leash. You might say he could afford to do so since, as these writers were hand-picked, he knew where they were coming from.

He himself, however, was no ideologue. On several occasions, he approved the argument I was making in a leader even though it was clear he didn't altogether agree with it. This was striking, since the leader column was supposedly his voice in the paper. On a number of issues, however, I came to the conclusion that he didn't really mind one way or the other as long as an intelligent argument was made – within the broad parameters of liberal or left-wing thinking, of course.

One of the more remarkable aspects of that leader room was the presence of Richard Gott, at various times the paper's foreign editor and features editor. Gott was not just any old lefty. When I worked at *The Guardian* he would come out with the most preposterous positions, such as his attempts to exonerate Pol Pot of his crimes against humanity.

Gott was afforded unlimited indulgence by Preston. The reason was said to be that theirs was a friendship which went back a very long way and Preston was loyal to his friends. But it was also, surely, that Gott was a man of immense charm, old-world courtesy, and erudition. He was clever and well-educated. He exuded the effortless superiority of Balliol college, Oxford; more pertinently, perhaps, he had a quality of lethal frivolity which stamped him as essentially an upper-class gadfly. It seemed to me that Preston was drawn to such types precisely because his own character was so different. Gauche, awkward, and shy, and trapped within a body permanently disabled and often plagued by pain from childhood polio, he tended to display a degree of sycophancy towards those who glittered with poise, confidence, and social clout.

Whatever the reason, Gott was indulged as if he were no more dubious than some kind of eccentric uncle. He would come out with support for one tyrannical left-wing figure or another and people would smile and roll their eyes in mock outrage. It was treated as a big joke. I was increasingly appalled – but I noted how even those who were similarly shocked (and there were more than a few) knew they had to keep their heads down. Gott was simply untouchable.

When many years later Gott was eventually outed as a KGB "agent of influence" Preston was devastated, talking about a deep betrayal of trust. But the fact was that Gott had made no secret of his opinions – and Preston had never displayed the slightest concern about such views, let alone removed him from the senior positions he held at the very heart of the paper. Indeed, others held similarly hard-left views, such as the chillingly Stalinist Jonathan Steele – who also served as foreign editor and a leader-writer – and, in later years, Seumas Milne, who at time of writing this book is Director of Strategy and Communications for the Labour party under its hard-left leader, Jeremy Corbyn. Although regarded with deep disapproval as a "tankie" – one who had supposedly supported the Soviet Union's invasion of Hungary and Czechoslovakia – Milne ran *The Guardian*'s op-ed pages for many years, offering a platform to apologists for terrorism, tyranny, and a denial of the very human rights to which *The Guardian* so ferociously nailed its flag.

That was possible because the soft left on the paper indulgently disavowed the hard left as essentially harmless ideological fossils. The hard left was deemed to have little continuity with nice, decent liberal lefties. But of course the double standard was egregious. While any expression of odious far-right views provoked instantaneous hysteria, denunciations, and general indignation, odious hard-left views provoked at most a few clicks of the tongue and world-weary disdain.

Moreover, while there were undoubtedly serious differences between them the distinction between tankie totalitarians and the soft left masked the fact that the soft left was also totalitarian in its instincts. It may have recoiled from the tanks rolling into Hungary or Czechoslovakia, but it most certainly parked its own tanks on the lawns of British society. From there it proceeded to lay siege to the fortresses of western culture, crushing all dissent beneath its tracks.

In 1982, I ran headlong into *The Guardian* tanks on, of all things, the issue of Israel. I say "of all things" because at that time I had never spoken or written about Israel. Indeed, I had never even been there and never wanted to go. I supported it in a vague kind of way as an unfortunate necessity, a refuge for Jews who were persecuted around the world. But that had nothing to do with me. I was British, a diaspora Jew happily living in the most civilized country on earth and working for its most civilized newspaper among some of the most civilized people one could hope to meet.

Nevertheless, I became extremely concerned about what seemed to be a vendetta at *The Guardian* and by the left in general against Israel. Given the current anti-Israel obsession in those quarters, it may be hard now to realize that it was not always thus. Indeed, before the Six Day War in 1967 *The Guardian* had been a passionate supporter of Israel. Along with the rest of the left, this attitude began to change in the seventies as the Palestinian leadership under Yasser Arafat, working in cahoots with the Soviet Union, started to develop its wildly successful propaganda strategy. This audaciously set out to rewrite history and, in the eyes of the left, transform the Israelis from socialist pioneers to colonialist aggressors and the Palestinians from genocidal aggressors into aboriginal victims.

For myself, I only began to notice that something was amiss during 1982. Even though until then I had hardly thought about Israel, I noticed that the way it was now being treated set it apart from any other country. Coverage of Israel had become disproportionate, distorted and viciously hostile, presenting it falsely as the bully in the region while ignoring or downplaying its victimization by the Arab world.

In a leader conference one day, I asked why *The Guardian* appeared to be pursuing a double standard in its coverage of the Middle East. Why did it afford next-to-no coverage of Arab atrocities against other Arabs while devoting acres of space to attacking Israel for defending itself against terrorism?

The answer I received from my colleagues that day stunned me. Of course there was a double standard, they said. How could there not be? The developing world did not subscribe to the same ethical beliefs as the west about the value of human life. The west therefore was not entitled to judge any mass killings in the developing world by its own standards. That would be racist.

However, they said, we regard Israel as being part of the West – so we do judge its actions by our standards. Furthermore, they added for good measure, you Jews tell us you are actually morally superior to the rest of us – so we are surely entitled to judge you by even higher standards.

I was most deeply shocked. The views they had just expressed amounted to pure racism. They were in effect saying that citizens of a developing country were not entitled to the same assumptions of human rights, life, and liberty as those in the developed world. What's more, the remarks they had made about Jews and moral superiority were not just wrong – since Jews believe they have particular and onerous moral duties in the world, not special status – but prejudiced and spiteful. And ominously, I had also been made to feel as if I was suddenly regarded as no longer one of them but something different, a Jew, just because I had questioned the double standard over Israel.

But how could this be? This was *The Guardian*, shrine of anti-racism, custodian of social conscience, embodiment of virtue. How then could such people be guilty of racism, and moreover dress it up as anti-racism?

Of course, this is the core of what we now know today as "political correctness" through which concepts are turned into their polar opposite in order to give miscreants a free pass if they belong to certain groups designated by the left as "victims." They are thus deemed to be incapable of doing anything wrong, while groups designated as "oppressors" can do no right.

According to this double-think it was simply impossible for the Guardian folk to be guilty of racism, since they championed the victims of the developing world against their western capitalist oppressors. But when those developing world unfortunates became the victims of the tyrants ruling over them, the left remained silent since to criticize any developing world person was said to be "racism."

This twisted thinking is what now passes for "progressive" thinking in Britain and America. Thus the left actually abandons the oppressed of the world to their fate, all the time weeping crocodile tears for them while sanctimoniously condemning "the right" for its heartlessness! It is this hijacking of language and thought itself that has done so much to destroy any common understanding of the political "center ground," the lethal confusion that has so unfortunately polarized political debate into vacuous caricatures that have precious little to do with reality.

The second shoe dropped that summer. In April, Britain had mounted a seaborne military campaign to retake the Falkland Islands from the invading Argentines. The controversy over this enterprise within *The Guardian* was all-consuming. The issue was uppermost in our minds. On June 7, 1982, forty-eight British troops were killed and 115 wounded when two landing craft were attacked. On June 14, the Argentines surrendered. Eight days earlier, on June 6, Israel had invaded Lebanon. At some point within that eight-day period, with the Falklands campaign reaching its denouement, I ran into *The Guardian*'s chief leader-writer, Geoffrey Taylor.

Taylor, who died in 2016, was the quintessential English gentleman. In his mild and tweedy diffidence, he could have stepped straight out of an Alan Bennett play. He was courteous, measured, and thoughtful. He was also the inspired wit who had created much of the wonderful San Serriffe spoof five years earlier. But he was also an Arabist. His default position, expressed in the most benign, gentle and civilized terms, was to sympathize with the Arabs and assume the worst about the behavior of Israel.

'Well, now, Melanie," he said to me that day in his donnish way, "what on earth are we going to say about your war?"

He was not referring to the Falklands. He was referring to Lebanon. "My" war was now a foreign war. I had suddenly become not really British, the outsider, the Jewish "other," all because I had dared protest at the injustice and worse in the paper's coverage of Israel.

At that moment, the iron entered my soul. Even so, it was to be many years before I would finally arrive at the conclusion which, with hindsight, should have been all too obvious right then. Deny it as I might, I had made myself different from people for whom no difference could be tolerated. Without realizing it at the time, I had stepped into a place from where there was never to be a way back.

Chapter 5

TRAITORS: HOW THE BATON WAS SNAPPED

Israel's invasion of Lebanon in 1982 to drive out the Palestine Liberation Organization, which had created a base for its terrorist activities there, unleashed what was at the time an unprecedented media onslaught upon Israel. I did not approve of that war and thought it was misguided, as it seemed to have been embarked upon with no clearly achievable end game in sight. But I was astounded to see that not only was Israel's victimization by Palestinian terrorism brushed aside but Israel was also being preposterously painted as the victimizer for seeking to protect its citizens from attack. I also noticed all around me something all too familiar crawling out, as if that war had opened Pandora's Box: classic Jew-hating images and concepts, dinner-party talk associating Jews with money, clannishness, and sinister power.

After the Israelis pulled out of Lebanon, this all gradually subsided. But I realized that what had been said to me at *The Guardian*, along with the wider onslaught of wildly distorted anti-Israeli and anti-Jewish invective, could not be dismissed. Yet I had been brought up with the belief that we Jews should be grateful to the British for having allowed us to settle in the UK, to assimilate and to prosper.

I couldn't get the images of that awful summer and autumn of 1982 out of my head, this eruption of a malign and vicious resentment in presenting Israelis as latter-day Nazis for seeking to defend themselves against attack. Nor could I sort out in my mind that my progressive *Guardian* colleagues thought it was anti-racist to deny the entitlement of human rights to the developing world, and regarded me in turn as not properly British just because I was a Jew who defended Israel.

I was also hearing something else. Any British Jew who protested that the unique singling out of Israel for this kind of double standard carried the unmistakable echoes of ancient Jew-hatred was accused of "waving the shroud of the Holocaust" and crying wolf over anti-Semitism. Jew-hatred had become the prejudice that dared not speak its name.

I tried to talk about this to my parents. My mother kept her views to herself, but my father was upset by the hostile coverage of Israel. I tried to explain what I thought was happening at *The Guardian*, that something horrible was taking place on the left where there seemed to be a refusal to accept that poor people could ever do anything wrong and where anti-Jewish feeling was coming out of the woodwork. This merely made my father more upset. He would not hear a word against his beloved *Guardian*.

As I continued to brood I happened to meet Julia Pascal, a playwright and theater director who felt as deeply about all this as I did. The result of our friendship was that I wrote a play distilling these experiences and dilemmas that Julia put on at a fringe theater in London, the Drill Hall, in January 1986.

The Drill Hall was a lesbian theatre, which might be thought a somewhat odd choice of venue for such a production. In fact, the theater's management clearly empathized with the plight of someone made to feel an outsider in her own society and they were magnificently supportive. I fear I subsequently caused them pain by some of the views I went on to express in later years, but that experience was very special and I will always be grateful for the support they gave me.

The play raised the issues of Jew-hatred in liberal English society, what patriotism meant to a British Jew, and how such a Jew could find personal equilibrium when such loyalty to Britain was publicly called into question by support for Israel.

In an interview about the play in 1986, I said, "Israel is becoming a pariah and I think that's going to continue... Jews aren't seen as victims or oppressed people at all. Jews are seen as people who victimize and oppress others...It's endemic, but there is an almost universal reluctance to admit this undercurrent of antisemitism exists, particularly among decent people who are wholly untainted by it. They simply will not accept it. It's as if one is striking at the very heart of what they believe their society to be about. You can see them almost physically recoil from the suggestion. Good liberals are more prepared to admit the British establishment and institutions are anti-black. But they are not prepared to admit the British establishment is anti-Jew."

I had stumbled on a phenomenon whose wider ramifications I would not fully grasp until the start of the next millennium. Michael Billington, *The Guardian*'s theater critic at the time, pooh-poohed what he thought was the play's shaky premise "...that a dithery, liberal English magazine would print a palpably inflammatory piece comparing the Israelis to Hitler and Himmler."

Thirty years on, it seems that liberal Britain never stops comparing the Israelis to the Nazis. It was not until the year 2000 that this issue would roar back into my life and all but engulf me. But the experiences of 1982 jolted me at that time in a far broader and profound way. They put me on notice that I had been wrong – wrong to have assumed that prejudice and bigotry were confined to the right, wrong to have assumed that I was just another member of the British liberal gang, wrong to have assumed that the liberal left was on the side of the angels. I now realized that, on the contrary, there was a gaping moral hole at its heart. From that point on, I began to look at the left across the board in a more detached and wary way.

Despite the events of 1982, I lived a charmed life during my first seven years at *The Guardian*. I was clearly marked out for great things. Preston described me in an article as a "corporal with a field-marshal's baton in her knapsack." For all that, however, and belied by my overconfident manner, I remained nervous, shy and – contrary to what was generally believed – consumed by self-doubt. Although at the time I had no insight into this, I can now see, in the light of all that subsequently happened, that I always felt myself to be an imposter, that I did not feel entitled to any of the praise or esteem that came my way because, as someone whose very life had caused my mother to be so unwell, I was really not entitled to exist at all.

In 1984, I became *The Guardian* news editor. This meant I was now in charge of my former colleagues, the news reporters, and the daily operation to obtain and write the news stories that would go into the following day's paper. It was a very big promotion. The news desk was the nerve center of the paper. The pressure would be intense and unrelenting.

By this stage I also had a second child: my daughter Abigail was born in 1982. To take on such a job with two very young children might be thought reckless. Somehow I managed every morning to fit in reading all the papers, listening to the news, and getting the children up, washed, and fed breakfast before the nanny arrived. Later, I even managed to fit in the school run. It was a military operation that left some male colleagues shaking their heads. I thought I had it licked.

The reporters, however, were bemused by my appointment; some were openly incredulous. I had been one of them – even as a leader-writer I had chosen not to move upstairs to the leader-room but remained at my desk in the newsroom – and I had no managerial experience whatsoever. I would now be under intense scrutiny, the focus of the gossip, backbiting, and sniping that were standard fare at *The Guardian*'s offices in Farringdon Road.

I was deeply dubious about the move. It meant I would have to forge a close working relationship with the senior sub-editors known collectively as the "backbench." Literally close; we all sat at the same table.

The backbench sub-editors were the production part of the editorial process, preparing the reporters' copy for publication. But the reporters regarded the backbench with deep suspicion and hostility because they rewrote the reporters' copy and often unilaterally altered the previously decided position of the stories in the paper.

The actual process of getting the copy from the reporters' typewriters into the paper was, to put it mildly, arcane. In the days before computers, reporters physically took their story, typed with two carbon copies, to the news desk and dropped it into wire baskets from where copies of each story were read and edited by the news desk staff and thence passed on, via the night news editor, to the backbench under the night editor, whose team often proceeded to undo all the editing work that had just been done.

I thought all this was completely bonkers. So, it seemed, did Peter Preston. I was urged to reform the system. I was also given the green light to tackle what Preston regarded as the endemic problem of the newsroom, the need to get rid of the dead wood among the reporters who he thought were taking the paper for a ride, and to sharpen and improve the reporting.

I told him I was nervous that, with this promotion, I would finally hit the limits of my own competence. "Not at all," he said cheerfully, puffing on his pipe, "it will be a terrific success."

In those days, I was an enormous fan of Peter Preston. I thought (and still do think) he was a journalistic genius. Despite his carefully cultivated opacity, I thought his professional instincts and insights were generally spot-on. I was always hearing people spitting tacks over his perceived duplicity, manipulation, and heartlessness. I just couldn't understand them. But then, I was his golden girl.

Before I actually took over as news editor, I had a month's "induction" shadowing the then holder of that post. On the very first day of my induction, I collapsed onto the floor. As I lay there dizzy and in pain, I heard the inevitable whispered speculation: "Do you think she's pregnant?" Ill as I was, I ground my teeth that at *The Guardian*, of all places, you couldn't be ill without also falling victim to an anti-feminist stereotype.

In fact, it turned out to be a chronic stomach condition almost certainly brought on by stress. And I hadn't even started in my new post. Little did I know it at the time, but it was to prove an augury of the ill health that would continuously plague me on the news desk.

I never thought I was cut out for that particular job; subsequent events proved that I was right. I didn't do it well and made many mistakes. Rapidly, I realized I was out of my depth; but instead of shouting for rescue, I slowly and silently drowned.

The worst mistake I made was to ignore the advice given right at the start by my predecessor, Peter Cole, who had been a brilliant success in the job. "Stick to what is possible," he said. "Keep everything ticking along, and whatever you do, don't try to bend the system to what you want it to do. Don't forget that Preston has never run a news desk; he hasn't got a clue what it involves."

I ignored that advice. Instead I decided that I would reform the desk structure and improve the standard of the journalism. This was a terrible misjudgment.

The first shock was to discover, as soon as I looked at the reporters' copy, how few of them could actually write. The quality of the writing on this "writers' newspaper" was often the outcome of the efforts of both the news desk and the reviled sub-editors.

Foolishly, I took it upon myself to try to remedy this situation. I thought if I could help the reporters improve their stories, I would short-circuit the sub-editors and everyone would be happy. Instead, I found myself resembling a British soldier on the Falls Road in Northern Ireland trying to keep the peace between Catholics and Protestants.

The reporters believed that every word they wrote was a gem. They resented any changes to their copy as desecration by philistines. The sub-editors held the reporters in almost total contempt as overeducated prima donnas; as often as not, they would blue-pencil the reporters' priceless prose and shoehorn into the story copy supplied by news agencies that they said was far superior in quality. The reporters looked to me to protect their every word from the predations of the sub-editors. The sub-editors looked to me to do one thing only – to keep the copy flowing in their direction regardless of what was in it. When I tried to preserve what was valuable in the reporters' copy, the subs treated me with contempt. When I tried to suggest ways in which their copy might be improved, the reporters treated me with contempt.

Others could and did manage such problems in that post far more effectively than I did. The key to it all was office politics, to which I was congenitally unsuited. It also didn't help that there seemed to be no common language between myself and the backbench. Theirs was a deeply macho culture. Their interests were football, cricket, and drinking, not necessarily in that order. Evenings were spent propping up the bar in the pub where they would stand, beer glass in hand, legs apart, and jingling coins in their pockets. I had never previously even been into a London pub. I joined them and drank fruit juice, always seemed to miss the cue at which someone else said "Another round? Here, let me…" and would soon be gasping for breath in the nauseating and then omnipresent fog of cigarette smoke.

Nor had I any knowledge of or interest in football or cricket. In desperation, the night editor, who for some reason had taken a shine to me, took me off for the day to a Test Match at Lord's in order to teach me the rules of cricket and thus provide me with the rudiments of communication. For the language of the backbench sub-editors was composed overwhelmingly of cricket metaphors, cryptic half-sentences, and in-jokes. Peter Preston, of course, habitually concealed his thinking like a squid squirting ink. As I shuttled unhappily between his office and the news desk, I felt as if I was ricocheting between the Mad Hatter's tea party and a sports club speaking Mandarin Chinese.

It would not be entirely accurate to say I had fallen victim to anti-woman prejudice. There were women on that desk who maneuvered around it without a problem; they could hold their own on the subject of football's First Division, and were themselves to be found in the pub sinking halves of bitter. But alas, even the trip to Lord's didn't turn me into one of the lads.

What also horrified me was the bent or craven nature of so much of the reporting. Whether for reasons of ideology or out of fear of upsetting their contacts, many of the reporters simply refused to do what I believed to be the essence of journalism: to follow where the evidence trail led you, dig out what someone didn't want you to know, and upset as many vested interests as possible in order to bring information to the public.

Instead, the political "lobby," the reporters who possessed the all-important parliamentary pass allowing them to stand at the entrance to the chambers of the Commons and Lords and thus gain access to politicians, were utterly resistant to doing anything that might break the rules of that exclusive club. So they tended to hunt in packs, deciding between them what the political story was even when it was actually something rather different, acting as conduits for politicians planting information, and refusing to write anything that might upset them.

Similarly, other specialist reporters were effectively the captives of their contacts. This was particularly true in education. By now, I had been looking for schools for my own children and I could see for myself that teaching had been hijacked by left-wing ideology. Instead of being taught to read and write, children were being left to play in various states of anarchy on the grounds that any exercise of adult authority was oppressive and would destroy the innate creativity of the child.

But when I tried to persuade the education team to tackle this, I hit a brick wall. Not only were they reluctant to challenge their contacts but, even more significantly, they just didn't see what I saw because they themselves wore the same left-wing blinkers as the educators who were the problem.

Some of the reporters were excellent: one whom I had hired, Peter Murtagh, won a press award for his investigative reporting. When he got his breakthrough on that story, he was so excited he phoned me and we met in a West End restaurant late one Saturday evening to exult together over his triumph. That was what I loved: breaking great stories, working with the reporters to develop and shape them, helping bring to the public news that no one else was telling them, feeling I was helping make a difference to the world for the better. Those were the good times.

But in the main, I knew it wasn't working. I had a wonderful deputy, upon whom I relied too much but who ultimately could not do what I myself needed to do. The newsroom dead wood remained unpruned. Preston made it clear that he was not going to remove anyone: I just had to make them work better. I hadn't managed to reform the desk structure. The power of the backbench was stronger than ever. The reporters were truculent, telling Preston that I needed to get a grip. They thought I was impossibly belligerent. In fact, I was being quietly treated for chronic panic attacks.

Why didn't I ask for help or to move to another post? Pride, certainly, but also fear. Preston had no time at all for anyone who displayed emotional or psychological fragility. I feared that if I displayed any such weakness, my charmed life at *The Guardian* would come to an abrupt end.

In 1987, I was put out of my misery. At that year's general election I ran, along with the very able junior news desk colleague who I had long suspected (correctly) was being groomed to replace me, three weeks of election coverage that was held to be a great success. After Mrs. Thatcher was elected for a third successive term as Prime Minister, Peter Preston took me out to lunch and fired me from the news desk.

It was done with all the tact and sensitivity for which staff relations at *The Guardian* were renowned. My new life was sketched out. I was to become an opinion columnist (a role regarded in those days with a certain contempt); I was to edit the regular advertising supplement on social policy, which, although lucrative, was little regarded; I was also to be invested with the title of Policy Editor, which I was informed was a very important role, even though as far as I could see there was to be no policy that I would actually edit.

When I inquired what being Policy Editor actually meant, I was told that if I didn't accept this deal that very important title would be conferred upon another named colleague who, as a result, would then be superior to me in the office pecking order. For once, there was no cloud of squirted ink, just brutal clarity.

When the news of my change of circumstance became known, Richard Gott – who despite his Olympian disdain for the petty bourgeoisie had always behaved kindly towards me – stopped by my desk. "Put out to grass with a column then," he said in grim sympathy. But if anyone thought that my writing would henceforth sink like a stone and drag me down with it into obscurity, they were about to be disabused.

Chapter 6

STUMBLING INTO THE CULTURE WARS

Not that I set out to make waves – far from it. What was about to happen took me entirely by surprise.

In my second column, I wrote in support of the introduction by the Conservative government of a deeply contentious national curriculum, which represented a desperate attempt to ensure that teachers actually started teaching children something at school. I wrote that, while the better-off could buy their way out of the system through living in leafy suburbs or sending their children to private schools, the poor were trapped by lousy local schools to which there was no alternative for their own children.

The reaction was instant and seismic. There was only one permitted explanation for the crisis in Britain's schools, and that was the spending cuts imposed by the heartless Thatcher government. To suggest that it might actually have had a point about the breakdown of teaching was simply unthinkable. Literally overnight, I became "right-wing." My *Guardian* colleagues gazed at me in perplexity and dismay. The fact that I had written with passion about the plight of poor people was totally disregarded. "This is a *Daily Mail* view," I was told, which was the greatest possible crime and insult since in such circles the *Mail* is considered to be so right-wing it is off the graph.

How had I reached this heretical position? By the staggering tactic of actually observing what was going on. I had looked at the local state-funded schools for my own young children and found them seriously wanting. This was not because they lacked money, but because the teachers had increasingly abandoned structured teaching. There were two decent primary schools in my area. I could get my children into neither because they were hugely over-enrolled. In the end I gave up and sent my children to independent schools. I could afford it; I knew most could not. As ever, I was concerned about those at the bottom of the heap.

Desperate parents and teachers intimidated by the education orthodoxy wrote to me in support. Friends and colleagues said I was a reactionary Gradgrind. Yet how could it be progressive to support an approach which inflicted its most devastating damage upon children at the bottom of the social heap, who depended absolutely on school to lift them out of disadvantage but who were being left ignorant, illiterate, and innumerate?

Galvanized by the reaction which suggested that things were far worse than I had realized, I wrote more about education. I wrote about the refusal to teach Standard English on the grounds that this was "elitist." How could this be? I had seen first-hand in my own undereducated family that an inability to control the language meant an inability to control their own lives. My Polish grandmother had not been able to fill in an official form without help; my father just didn't have the words to express complicated thoughts, and would always lose out against those who looked down at him from their educated pedestal.

I also observed that those putting such pressure on these teachers from the education establishment were the supercilious upper-middle classes, who had no personal experience whatsoever of what it was actually like to be poor and uneducated or an immigrant but were nevertheless imposing their own ideological fantasies onto the vulnerable and harming them as a result. Teachers wrote to me in despair at the pressure not to impose Standard English on children on the grounds that this was discriminatory. They knew that, on the contrary, this was to abandon those children to permanent servitude and ignorance.

Late that same year I wrote about how black parents in inner London were cheering on the government's education reforms; they despaired of a system which they thought had so grievously failed two generations of black children. But at the so anti-racist *Guardian*, the views of those black parents simply counted for nothing. The left-wing Inner London Education Authority could never be wrong; the Tory government could never be right.

In 1990 I wrote that deteriorating education standards had little to do with low pay for teachers or schools starved of money. It was teachers and teaching that made the difference to children's lives. The problem was the number of bad teachers who were turning good teachers into a beleaguered minority, in what I described as "the vicious circle of an education establishment that perpetuates its own myths down through generations of poorly taught children" (*The Guardian*, March 2, 1990).

Reaction to this column was so extreme that I devoted a further piece to it alone. There, I recorded that in the space of two weeks I had been described as "ignorant, silly, intellectually vulgar, vicious, irresponsible, elitist, middle-class, fatuous, dangerous, intemperate, shallow, strident, reactionary, near-hysterical, propagandist, simplistic, well-paid, unbalanced, prejudiced, rabid, venomous, and pathetic." Three-quarters of the letters I received had been hostile. Traditional teaching was equated with drilling, Dickens, and the "new right," and my real crime was to have dared to air such arguments at all.

But it was the letters of support that were the most startling and shed a devastating light on the situation they described as "insanity." One educational psychologist wrote: "I greet with relief the beginning of debate about modern teaching practices. In my job I see small children whose listening skills and ability to stay focused on a task are chronic – yet they are put to learn in an environment which no undergraduate would have to suffer…. Sometimes a brave teacher does arrange the tables so that each child has a space of his or her own; the children love it, but the teacher has to move the tables back again. Children do not learn through play…but through instruction, explanation, guidance, motivation from an adult. Children need to be taught to make connections, to look for meanings. They do not learn from Wendy houses or from computers, they learn from people. And whenever I say this to a group of teachers, the older and wiser members of the group come to me afterwards and thank me for saying it; they have been waiting for years for someone to make this point. But for some reason they cannot say this in public. And neither can I; which is why I do not want my name published. My job is important to me, and public condemnation of teaching methods will not be approved. But in an odd way, I cannot really pinpoint who will disapprove" (*The Guardian*, March 26, 1990).

When I saw that particular letter, a chill came over me. It was at that point that I realized something very bad indeed was happening to Britain. What was being described was more akin to life in a totalitarian state. Dissent was being silenced, and those who ran against the orthodoxy were being forced to operate in secret; worse still, the very meaning of concepts such as education, teaching and knowledge was being unilaterally altered, and thousands of children, particularly those at the bottom of the social heap, were being abandoned to ignorance and institutionalized disadvantage.

If ever there was an abuse of power for journalists to investigate, this was surely it. For most of my colleagues, however, it was I who was out of step. In due course, a couple of more independent-minded thinkers successively took on the education reporting brief and so on each occasion I had an ally in the newsroom. It was nevertheless still very much, at any one time, only the two of us *contra mundum*.

It was not just my professional world which in 1987 started to crack apart. For some time, I had been aware that something seemed to be badly troubling my mother. My father also seemed to be suffering: there was clearly some kind of unspoken problem between them. In June 1987 they were to celebrate their 40th wedding anniversary. I was planning to hold a party for them in our garden, but my mother was being difficult about this: disengaged, even churlish. As I had always done, I internalized the anxiety and trod gingerly around the usual eggshells to avoid provoking the always-feared collapse.

One Saturday afternoon, when they came for tea as they did every week, I finally snapped. I begged her to end the secrecy and tell me just what was going on. And so in a flat voice she told me. Three years previously, her neurologist had finally told her the true nature of her "condition." After treating her for 25 years he was now retiring from practice, and he chose this final consultation to tell her that her "condition" was multiple sclerosis.

How could this possibly have happened? For the neurologist to have kept this from her meant there must have been in turn a conspiracy of secrecy for a quarter of a century between him, her general practitioner, her psychiatrist and everyone else who had treated her. She had never been told what was actually wrong with her until the day her neurologist dumped this knowledge on her and then abandoned her. How could he have been so cruel?

Yet maybe he had thought that if he put the correct name to her "condition" she might not have been able to cope. And very likely that was correct. My parents knew everything about each other, told each other everything, lived inside each other's skins. Yet after she learned her true diagnosis, she told no one and kept it secret from my father for a year; and they both kept it from me for a further two years, until I wrenched it out of her.

What a dreadful and cruel irony, that someone who did not recognize the boundaries between herself and others should have fallen victim to an autoimmune disease in which the body destroys friendly organisms while embracing those that will attack it. My mother had always needed to maintain total control over matters that should not have concerned her, such as the way she somehow managed to make all relationships between her immediate family members pass through her rather than take place between each other; now she was to lose control over one after another of her own bodily functions. As a child, I had inappropriately been "parentified" by infantilized parents; now my mother was indeed to become dependent and I was to become her caregiver. Fate had turned what had previously been a set of destructive fantasies into a hideous reality.

From that moment, it seemed, my mother was caught in a downward spiral that, over the following seventeen years when she also developed Parkinson's disease and vascular dementia, was to rob her progressively of mobility, vision, control of her bodily functions and eventually her mind.

There are people who, faced with a devastating and progressive disease, refuse to go under. They constantly adapt and, taking every day as it comes, manage to extract from the world around them every ounce of life. My mother was not one of them. Faced with the truth about her illness, she went under. She reacted as she had always done to anything which threatened her carefully controlled world: she pretended it wasn't so.

The result was that she refused to accept the help or aids that were offered to her. Without adequate assistance, she allowed her illness to take over. And as her world shrank into a space defined exclusively by her disease, an intolerable burden was dumped on my father. In those terrible years, he looked after her with spaniel-like devotion. Refusing to accept a walker, my mother would shuffle around the flat clinging onto a wooden tea-trolley for support. And my father would follow a few paces behind, ready to catch her if she should fall.

The experience of those years also told me that something was going very wrong with the welfare state. It wasn't just the lack of provision, which meant that the only care available for my mother from the local authority was a few hours a week with untrained caregivers who had been recruited off the street. It was also a callousness and indifference amongst the supposedly caring services. It was the hospital nurses who, when my mother broke her hip and through her feebleness was unable to move at all in her hospital bed, left her food and water unwrapped or out of reach and refused to make her comfortable; and the ward sister who, when I complained, told me with a straight face that my mother, who could barely put one foot in front of the other, had a short time before been "skipping around the ward."

I realized then that in the National Health Service, Britain's sanctified temple of altruism, compassion, and decency, if you were old, feeble and poor you just didn't stand a chance.

Melanie's parents, 1940s

Zaida, *Booba*, Marie and Betty, 1940s

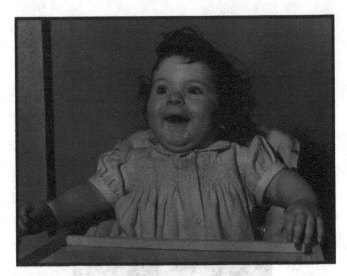

A few months old

With Mabel, 1951

With Alfred, 1957

With Joshua, Wadham Ball, 1969

Melanie at Joshua's graduation, Oxford, 1972

Graduation ceremony, University of Oxford, 1973

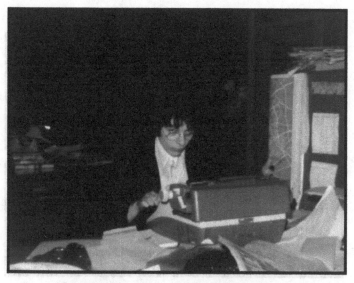

Working at the *Evening Echo*, Hemel Hempstead, 1975

Young Journalist of the Year, 1975, with Ivor Lewis, Melanie's editor

Reporter of the Year Award, Presented by Margaret Thatcher

Melanie's Reporter of the Year 1980 acceptance speech

Melanie reading her profile in *The Independent*, 2005

Question Time, BBC Television, 2013. L-R: Russell Brand, Tessa Jowell, Boris Johnson, David Dimbleby, Ed Davie, Melanie

Chapter 7

ONWARDS INTO THE FIRE

The ineluctable logic of what I was discovering led me step by step in a direction I had never imagined I would take. There was no sudden break, no thunderclap of revelation, no seismic life-changing event. It wasn't even that I was simply growing older. My views steadily evolved, building block by building block on the scaffolding of my own belief in truth and evidence and morality, from one issue to another until an entirely new structure seemed to arise. But it wasn't actually new at all. It was standing on the same firm foundations, while the citadels of western belief and identity were crumbling one by one.

Although at the time I didn't realize it, I was also stepping outside a basic journalistic convention on highbrow papers. Most such rarefied journalists write for other journalists or to impress politicians or other members of the great and the good. By contrast, I always wrote for ordinary people. But the left didn't like ordinary people and in particular the lower middle class, the striving class who believed in things like self-discipline and personal responsibility.

I did not dislike them. I remained one of them. Just as they were skeptical of intellectual abstractions, fantasies or utopian solutions, so I was too. I simply went where the evidence led. "Leftish intellectuals," I wrote, "too often have such contempt for the views of the populace at large, such a terror (not wholly unjustified) that popular prejudice owes nothing to facts that they sometimes appear to think that the only people either worth listening to or talking to are themselves" (*The Guardian*, January 13, 1989).

According to my own logic, I was trapping myself. By merely writing this, I was becoming for those leftish intellectuals someone not worth listening or talking to. The more I connected with reality and championed the people against the left, the more I sealed my own fate.

Issue by issue, my writing during the 1980s and 1990s reflected the fact that Britain was undergoing a cultural revolution. And as society changed, so too did my own attitudes change. Fundamental assumptions and values were being challenged, attacked and undermined. The homogeneity of British society was being eroded by mass immigration, which was changing the face of the country. As socialism withered and the free market dominated, identity politics replaced economics. Above all, what was emerging was the cult of the individual, which gave rise to the dominance of subjective experience over objective authority of any kind. This was not merely to transform family life, but also turn the understanding of what was normal and what transgressive inside out.

My ideals remained as they had always been: upholding truth over lies, justice over injustice, protecting the weak against the strong, putting others first instead of the self. One by one, however, every one of these ideals was being smashed by my former comrades on the left in their relentless march through the institutions. Issue by issue I felt they were embracing lies over truth, injustice over justice, rule by the strong over the weak, and even destroying the very basis of what it was to be a human being.

My position was not so much political as moral. The left was rejecting all external authority and embracing instead moral and cultural relativism, the idea that "what is right" is "what is right for me," and declaring any hierarchy of values illegitimate. But to me, this was a recipe for an amoral free-for-all in which freedom would die and the most vulnerable would go to the wall. This was not progressive; this was going to take us backwards towards a Hobbesian war of all against all.

So, departing from the orthodoxy on such varied issues as the underclass, embryo research, human rights, volunteering and multiculturalism, I pressed on further and further into the fire. One particular issue, however, suddenly propelled me in left-wing eyes into yet another circle of hell.

In the late eighties, environmentalism emerged as the latest great progressive cause. Suddenly people were fulminating about pollution, extinction of species, the felling of the rainforests, the hole in the ozone layer and man-made global warming, as a result of which the planet was heading for destruction.

Right from the start, I smelled charlatanry. I cared about curbing pollution and protecting wildlife, and believed very strongly that people had a duty to safeguard the environment. But I thought that this new creed smacked of zealotry. Indeed, some of the claims being made by the greens, such as the belief that the planet had an anthropomorphic identity as the goddess Gaia, struck me as totally off the wall. And as for man-made global warming, it was immediately obvious – and this was before we learned about the brazen scientific frauds that were perpetrated to prop up the theory – there was simply no evidence that anything out of the historical ordinary was happening to the climate at all.

Worse, I saw that deep green environmentalism brought together deeply obnoxious strands of thinking on both left and right. On the left, it was very obviously a new take on the usual anti-Western, anti-capitalist agenda; the West would have to give up consumerism and return to a barter economy to save the planet. Or something like that. But it was also a sanitized version of the disreputable and discredited dogma of population control, which had given rise to the eugenics movement and the semi-mystical worship of the organic, both of which had been deeply implicated in both the rise of Nazism and in "progressive" thinking up to World War II.

To me, the clear message of environmentalism was that the planet would be fine if it wasn't for the human race. So it was a deeply regressive, reactionary, proto-fascist movement for putting modernity into reverse, destroying the integrity of science and threatening humanity itself.

Even more significantly, it also showed me the artificiality of the distinction between left and right. It simply wasn't true that the left was fighting the good fight for progress against reaction, for reason against obscurantism, for humanity against fascism. No, environmentalism placed the left on the other side of these divisions. And yet it was axiomatic that environmentalism was a left-wing cause and synonymous with virtue, and anyone who opposed it was a rapacious, reactionary right-winger in hock to Big Oil.

So it was a particularly delicious development when Peter Preston, with his genius for spotting a cultural trend significant enough to engender a swathe of lucrative advertising, decided to start a new supplement, *Environment Guardian*, and asked me to be its editor. When I reminded him what my views were, his eyes glittered with amusement. Maybe he thought a spot of controversy wouldn't be bad for business.

Friends of the Earth and Greenpeace were thrilled to learn that *The Guardian* was starting such a supplement and doubtless thought they would turn it into their house journal. When they learned of the views of its editor, however, they were aghast and stupefied. Or so I was told by my gifted and creative deputy John Vidal who, despite being himself a deeply committed green, was loyal and professional to a fault. Between us, we managed to turn out an environment supplement which asked many important questions while managing to steer clear of the rocks of wilder eco-zealotry.

By far my biggest break with the left – the most visceral, the most ferocious, the cultural Rubicon – was over the breakdown of the family.

In the late 1980s, I noticed that the institution of the family was suffering a "chronic crisis of identity and self-confidence." There were more and more divorces and single parents; at the same time parents were becoming less confident in managing their children. Poverty, the left's habitual excuse, could not be the culprit since middle-class children were also not receiving from their parents the attention they required. "Many children lack a consistent mother or father figure," said researchers from Goldsmith's College, London ("How to avoid children growing up like Lord of the Flies?" *The Guardian*, July 15, 1988).

As ever, I was listening to the evidence of those with no ideological dog in the fight but who simply spoke of what they saw was happening. In 1990, both the Conservative government minister, Kenneth Baker, and his ideological opponent, Mary Tuck, the liberal former head of research at the Home Office, held fatherless families at least partly responsible for a national breakdown in authority and rising levels of crime. Zelda West-Meads of the marriage guidance counselors Relate got to the heart of the issue when she said that, although many single mothers did a heroic job, it was the absence of the father that did such terrible damage to their children. This was because children drew for their own identity from the combination of male and female components of their family. Even with a loving mother, children without their father felt torn in two. "The denial of these inconvenient truths," I wrote, "derived from the instinct for self-justification rather than care for the interests of children" (*The Guardian*, May 11, 1990).

The balloon really went up, however, with a report in 1991 about the effects of family breakdown by two social scientists, Norman Dennis and George Erdos, that included a foreword by the doyen of sociologists and promoter of left-wing educational doctrine, A.H. Halsey.

There was incontrovertible evidence, according to Dennis and Erdos, that children in fractured family units tended to die earlier, suffer more ill health, do less well at school, were more likely to be unemployed, more prone to criminal behavior and to repeat as adults the same cycle of unstable parenting.

The report provoked uproar. The reason was not just what it said but who was saying it; for although the report had been published by the right-wing Institute of Economic Affairs, the authors were from the left. Indeed, Halsey and Dennis were co-authors of the classic work *English Ethical Socialism*, and regarded themselves as still belonging to the tradition when the left famously owed "more to Methodism than to Marx." But being "against single mothers," as this was crudely seen, was an evil right-wing position. It was therefore simply impossible for the authors to be left-wing. They were therefore instantly rebranded right-wing. But since they clearly were not, they could not easily be dismissed; and so the uproar continued.

The social science establishment circled the wagons. One distinguished academic claimed the authors' research was "old, out-of-date, selective, and misleading." I rang this expert to ask what the research actually said. But when pressed, he would not answer the question. Instead he released a stream of invective, calling the authors' mental faculties into question and asking emotionally, "What do these people want? Do they want unhappy parents to stay together?"

Eventually, he admitted that the authors were actually correct as far as the research was concerned. But, he asked rhetorically, where had that got anyone? Nowhere! Was it possible to turn back the clock? Of course not! And why were they so concerned about the rights of the child? What about the rights of the parents? (*Tablet*, July 31, 1993).

Of course, he himself turned out to be divorced. That conversation revealed a devastating pattern that I was to encounter over and over again. Truth was being sacrificed to expediency. Evidence would be denied if the consequences were too inconvenient. Sheer selfishness was being justified regardless of the damage done to others.

Surely, though, the essence of being progressive was to minimize harm and protect the most vulnerable? Yet this was simply tossed aside by left-wingers, who elevated their own desires into rights that trumped the emotional, physical and intellectual well-being of their children – and then berated as heartless reactionaries those who criticized them!

The more this was being justified, the more it was happening. Rising numbers of people were abandoning their spouses and children, or breaking up other people's families, or bringing children into the world without a father around at all. The left claimed that these activities made the women and children happy and were a refreshing change from the bad old days when simply everyone was miserable because marriage chained women to men who, as everyone with the correct view knew for a fact, were basically feckless wife-beaters and child abusers as well as being irrationally prejudiced against the opposite sex.

Yet there was a huge amount of evidence that, in general, family disintegration and reformation did incalculable damage to children and that there was far greater risk of abuse of children or violence between adults in cohabiting or serial relationships. Since marriage, by and large, was a protection for both children and adults I thought the state should promote it as a social good. For this I was told I was reactionary, authoritarian and, of course, right-wing. Yet how could it be progressive to encourage deceit, betrayal of trust, breaking of promises and harm to children?

I talked to other experts and looked at the evidence. It was unequivocal: in general, and relatively speaking, divorce, step-parenting and lone parenthood hurt children. A child psychiatrist, Dr. Sebastian Kraemer, told me he regarded it as "a personal holocaust for the children when the parents separate…I see it clinically that children are deeply hurt, their lives are shattered because the people who got together to make them can't keep together to bring them up" (*The Guardian*, September 16, 1991).

Later, Dr. Kraemer told me he regretted having said this; widespread family breakdown was now an established feature of society, and we all had to accept it and work out how to make the best of it. Over and over again I found that family therapists, academics and other experts were in effect censoring themselves over the baleful effects of family breakdown, either because they felt it was a social tide that could not be resisted or because, increasingly, they or their own families were themselves caught up in it.

As far as I was concerned, this was selling the pass and abandoning the vulnerable. There was surely an overriding duty to tell the truth about the damage being done by fragmented family life, consequences that were harming not just children but also women and men. But those who did tell the truth as they found it risked becoming victims of a professional witch-hunt.

Two researchers from Exeter University's Department of Child Health, Dr. John Tripp and Monica Cockett, discovered that although children whose parents were fighting each other did worse than children from peaceful intact families, they did worse still after their parents had divorced (*Exeter Family Study: Family Breakdown and Its Impact on Children*, University of Exeter Press, 1994). This was explosive, since a major justification for easier divorce was the claim that children were usually better off if their unhappy parents separated.

From the moment they published their research, the authors found themselves bad-mouthed and their report rubbished by influential academics, and they were cut off from further funding. One academic on a grant-making body told me their work was "methodologically unsound;" the evidence for this claim, however, seemed to be merely that they "had an agenda" merely because one of them was a committed Christian (*Observer*, June 28, 1998).

When I started writing about the baleful effects of family breakdown, I was accosted angrily by someone I had previously thought of as a friend. "How can you possibly say that family breakdown hurts children?" he spat out at me. "The worst damage to a child is always done by the traditional nuclear family!"

I could only gaze at him, defeated by the sheer impossibility of conveying the stupendous shallowness of such an attitude. I, of all people, knew firsthand what damage and anguish could be inflicted within an apparently model family. But I also knew that much of what I had experienced or witnessed derived from the absence of a properly involved father. I had personal knowledge of the lifelong harm inflicted on a child who is forced to become, in effect, the parent to her own parent. I knew intimately what harm can be done to a child's psyche from a dyadic relationship with one parent, unmediated and unmitigated by the other. I knew from experience how the absence of proper fathering could screw up a child for life. How then could my erstwhile friend or anyone else possibly be sanguine about the explosion of lone parenting, female-headed households and mass fatherlessness?

On issues such as education and family, I believed I was doing no more than stating the obvious. To my amazement, however, I found that I was now branded an extremist for doing so. Astoundingly, truth, evidence and reason had become right-wing concepts. I was now deemed to have become "the right" and even "the extreme right." And when I started writing about family breakdown, I was also called an "Old Testament fundamentalist."

At the time, I shrugged this aside as merely a gratuitous bit of bigotry. Much later, however, I came to realize that it was actually a rather precise insult. My assailants had immediately understood something I did not myself at the time understand: that the destruction of the traditional family had as its real target the destruction of Biblical morality. I thought I was merely standing up for evidence, duty and the protection of the vulnerable. But they understood that the banner behind which I was actually marching was the Biblical moral law which put chains on people's appetites.

The result was a kind of social ostracism. Gradually I noticed that I was no longer being invited to join colleagues for lunch, no longer receiving invitations to parties at their houses, no longer getting the flow of gossipy messages and office banter that had once made me feel as if I was back in an Oxford junior common room. Now, at lunchtimes, I found the office emptying around me. Few ever tried to engage me in argument. I simply became more and more isolated.

Something similar was happening outside the office too. Gradually, my more politically minded friends drifted away. From snatches of their conversation, I deduced that what had finally got to them above all was my position on family breakdown. I realized that they took it personally, those who themselves had walked out on their families or were cheating on their spouses. Some of them said to me they felt I was disapproving of what they had done.

But much of the time, I had no idea at all what they had done. And in any event, I was not judging individuals (except where I knew someone really had behaved badly). Of course there were divorced or lone parents who behaved in a responsible and caring manner. I was merely writing about general patterns of relative harm, the only way one could write about public policy. Why couldn't they understand this?

I had not yet realized that the left's aggression towards any dissent or challenge is essentially defensive. They are either guilty about what they are doing because they know it is wrong, or else at some level at least they know that their intellectual position is built on sand. What matters to them above all is that they are seen to be virtuous and intelligent. They care about being seen to be compassionate. They simply cannot deal with the possibility that they might not be. They deal with any such suggestion not by facing up to any harm they may be doing but by shutting down the argument altogether. That's because the banner behind which they march is not altruism. It is narcissism. But it took me a very long time fully to grasp this.

And in due course, what I saw so clearly in the areas of education or family, which was in essence the displacement of truth by ideology, I would come to realize was part of a much bigger picture. But it took me a long time to put it all together and arrive at that conclusion. And that was because I was unwilling to accept the great breach to which my own logic would inexorably lead me.

Chapter 8

JOURNALISM IN TRANSITION

While the tectonic plates of British society were shifting, *The Guardian* was experiencing its own cultural transition. Journalism itself was having its post-modern moment. Truth was now said to be an illusion; objectivity was a sham; journalists who tried to be dispassionate were therefore perpetrating a fraud upon the public. The only honest approach was for journalists to wear their hearts on their sleeves; this was not to be called bias, but honesty.

This doctrine was called "the journalism of attachment." To me, however, it was a green light for journalists to tell lies, disseminate propaganda, and make it all up. There were some notable examples of this at *The Guardian* in those years. Those stories, most of which centered on the Bosnian War, caused controversy within the paper with critics pointing out that certain events they described did not actually happen. To which the answer was that they told "the broader truth." This "broader truth" seemed instead to me to be a lie.

Shocked as I was by this, I was no less dismayed by a parallel development: the steady slide of the paper down-market. Again, it reflected a broader trend across the press; but we were

The Guardian and supposed to be immune from that kind of pressure. Nevertheless, stories and articles became shorter, more trivial and, in my view, less authoritative and accurate.

In 1988, the paper was redesigned to look more modern and fashionable. The unease this stirred, however, was as nothing compared to what happened four years later when the paper launched a supplement called *G2*. It was trivial, flip and in-your-face; the serious articles it also contained were all but overlooked in the storm over "dumbing down" that then ensued. But the traditionalists were hopelessly outgunned. Other papers immediately copied its stylish innovations. It was in fact a brilliant concept, brilliantly executed. Its creator was Alan Rusbridger.

I was bereft. The paper appeared to be lurching away from the high-minded journalistic ideals of which it was supposedly the custodian. And this was made all the more bitter because I was now excluded from its inner counsels, beached in the backwaters of environment and social policy, no longer even part of the collegiate camaraderie that once would have seen me sloping off with colleagues for lunch in a local cafe.

It would be nice to record that in these circumstances I behaved with forbearance and circumspection. Alas, this would not even be a "broader truth." I made a nuisance of myself, desperately trying to get a hearing for my protests that the paper was losing its soul. Looking back, I am embarrassed by such apparent arrogance. I can only say that at the time I felt like a little rowing boat being pounded by gales and giant waves while the mother ship had cast me adrift and was now sailing full steam ahead over the horizon.

Into this emotional maelstrom came a blow to the solar plexus. Out of the blue, Preston suggested I should become the paper's Middle East correspondent and move to Israel. Given how closely I am identified with Israel's cause today, it may seem strange that I should have taken this so amiss. But at that time I had never even been to Israel. My concern for the country was based merely on a profound sense of injustice and an acute ear to the lessons of history, not a personal identification with what was to me an entirely foreign and indeed somewhat unappealing place.

More to the point, my entire journalistic career had been spent writing about British domestic issues. I had no experience in foreign affairs whatsoever. Preston knew that better than anyone. So the offer didn't feel like an offer at all. It felt like a dispatch into exile: an exile, moreover, with a twist.

For this was not a proposal to send me on some random foreign posting. It was to send me to one particular country, Israel, on the implicit grounds that I had a particular interest in that country. And on what was the assumption of that interest based? A few remarks to colleagues about the strange obsession of the left with Israel – and of course, my play. But that was it. I had never written about Israel. It was not a place to which I had ever expressed a wish to go. Maybe Preston really did think he was doing me a kindness. But to me, it felt as if I was being punished not just for being troublesome but being a troublesome Jew.

I refused the offer and remained in London. There were no repercussions; the subject was never mentioned again.

It was perhaps at that moment, however, that it really hit home. I was being cut loose. But I still couldn't bear to let go.

Chapter 9

END TIMES AT THE GUARDIAN

The great fight over the family had crystallized the culture wars for me. Demonstrable harm was being done to children, and so-called progressives were complicit in widening and deepening that harm. Now other thinkers started to notice that the social glue was coming unstuck and that the great alibi of poverty just didn't wash. There were voices on the left who not only said this was wrong, but believed that the left itself had gone terribly wrong. It was these people who influenced me most because they came from a tradition that was my own – a belief in restraining self-interest out of a duty to others, in taking responsibility for one's actions, in caring for the vulnerable. All essential to make a better world. All supposedly virtues of the left, but all now being repudiated by the left.

I was influenced by writers such as David Selbourne, the political philosopher who was himself hounded out of his teaching post at Ruskin college, Oxford, after writing an article in *The Times* in 1986 on corruption in the Labour politics of Liverpool. Writing during the "Wapping dispute," in which members of the print unions were at loggerheads with the newspaper's proprietor Rupert Murdoch, Selbourne was accused both by students and colleagues at Ruskin of having betrayed union interests by publishing the article in a Murdoch paper. His lectures were picketed by print-union members and militant students and he was prevented from teaching. Selbourne's unsparing analysis of Britain's loss of moral order, allied to the thuggish treatment he received at the hands of so-called progressives, reinforced and helped explain what I was seeing unfold before me: that the left had lost the moral plot.

I was also influenced by the ethical socialist and grand old man of sociology A.H. Halsey, hitherto an icon of the left but who was now being treated preposterously as a pariah of the right on account of his magisterial warnings about family breakdown and the importance of marriage. Not only that, but this one-time guru of progressive education theories was now denouncing the "mindless egalitarianism" that was leaving children ignorant and untaught.

Halsey had never denied the importance of tradition or authority, he said; he had merely wanted the ability of poor children to be recognized and developed. But this had been overtaken by a "sub-Marxist message" that there weren't any standards at all, a movement that had captured the teacher-training colleges. As for the family, Halsey told me that the decline of the traditional family was the "cancer in the lungs of the modern left...The Conservatives injected rampant individualism into economic policy, and the left called it greed. But the left injected the same rampant individualism into family relations and called it progress" (*The Guardian*, February 23, 1993).

I had come to exactly the same conclusion; here was one of the icons of the left validating my own view. What he was describing was the eclipse of "ethical socialism," the moral movement of social progress on the left whose goal was to create a better society, by a sub-Marxist ideology whose revolutionary goal was the destruction of that society and its replacement by a quite different one. Correctly, he identified that the left had become the sum of various interest groups all out for their own particular causes such as single parenthood, homosexuality, or animal rights.

For him as for me, the family was the issue of issues because the traditional family embodied the idea that there was something beyond the selfish individual. It was thus a "sacred institution." Yet now it was being turned into a mere contract which either side could break more or less at will. Halsey understood that this kind of self-centered individualism contained the seeds of the left's own destruction, and the destruction of Western society.

Tellingly, the response of the modern left to Halsey was to say he had "gone gaga." As I had already learned, when challenged the left does not come up with a counter-argument. It just demonizes. And the suggestion of insanity, as in the former Soviet Union, is its principal branding of choice.

My own writing now became increasingly hard-edged. Once the spell of the left was broken and I saw that it was actually promoting harm and describing that harm as progressive, first in its refusal to condemn developing world tyrants and then over education and the family, I began to see the same pattern repeated again and again. The more the left demonized those who were restating moral precepts based on duty rather than self-interest, the more important it became to me to try to open people's eyes to what was thus being ignored, misrepresented or denied.

I worried, for example, about the "moral myopia" through which cannibalism, child mutilation and bestiality were becoming the cinema's stock-in-trade. Why was it, I asked, that we seemed to lurch from one extreme to another, from censorship to license with nothing in between? (*The Guardian*, March 12, 1993). Authority was being disastrously confused with authoritarianism, I lamented, and turned into a taboo along with individual responsibility and the nuclear family; the effects were all around us in rampant juvenile crime (*The Guardian*, March 5,1993).

The fragmentation of the family was leading to the fragmentation of moral values, but any attempt to tell people how they should behave was being damned as "theoretical imperialism" while telling them that lifestyle choice was the only acceptable doctrine was not (*The Guardian*, April 3, 1993). In May 1993, after a single mother treated with a fertility drug gave birth to sextuplets, I was aghast at the "reckless amorality" of a society that had reached its "grotesque apogee" when "no fewer than 37 hard-pressed health service employees – three obstetricians, two pediatric consultants, three anesthetists, four pediatric registrars, five senior midwives, five senior house officers, two pharmacists, a radiologist, and twelve nurses – shared general jubilation for the brilliant masterstroke of creating a single-parent family of seven" (*The Guardian*, May 28, 1993).

That was my last column for *The Guardian*.

Chapter 10

THE WORST WITCH IN THE HUNT

In 1993, *The Guardian* bought the *Observer*, then an ailing Sunday newspaper. It did so largely in order to stymie the *Independent*, which had branched out into the *Independent on Sunday* and was thus posing ever more of a threat. There also seemed to be an obvious confluence of viewpoints, since the *Observer* was a distinguished liberal paper. The then-deputy editor of *The Guardian*, Jonathan Fenby, was appointed editor of the *Observer* and he asked me to join him as a columnist. In June 1993 I duly moved to the *Observer* offices in Battersea, where it was based until it moved into offices above *The Guardian* in Farringdon Road.

Joining the *Observer* seemed a reasonable response to my dilemma. I now felt so much out on a limb at *The Guardian* that I knew I had to move on, but I could not bring myself to leave it altogether. So the *Observer* seemed to offer a very timely halfway house, even though I was uneasily aware that Fenby's approach might well have been at Preston's behest.

For a while, it worked very well. Fenby was genial, serious-minded and with no animosity towards me. The *Observer* was a paper with a long, classically liberal tradition and at that time was still demonstrably a liberal newspaper. It was benign and tolerant in outlook, and did not appear to be marked by the bitterness and malice of *The Guardian*. There were undoubted tensions: Fenby brought in some people from the *Independent*, where he had previously worked, and there was a certain amount of jostling and rivalry. But I liked the generosity of spirit of the old *Observer* hands. Fenby was unfailingly supportive, if distracted, and the columns I wrote were sharper as if I felt more confident.

I wrote in despair about the crisis of belief within the Labour party, which viewed support for the EU Maastricht Treaty as progressive even though this significant erosion of national sovereignty within Europe would destroy jobs and promote social disharmony, racism and xenophobia (*Observer*, June 6, 1993). This was becoming unsayable; the Tory party itself was demonizing the opponents of Maastricht as swivel-eyed fanatics. It was axiomatic that support for the EU was not only the correct progressive position but had become the political center ground, even though a decade earlier it had been progressive to be hostile to the EU.

I wrote about the crucial importance of fathers to the emotional health of children, and pleaded that people should stop being frightened to say that the traditional family was best for children's welfare (*Observer*, June 13, 1993). By now, it seemed to me that family breakdown was simply dissolving the bonds of society and civilization itself. I was reporting on whole communities where committed fathers were now almost totally unknown. Children as young as five were becoming highly sexualized from the example of their promiscuous mothers. Teachers, doctors and social workers were horrified by the way in which both left and right were ignoring or misrepresenting this disaster: gross individual and social degradation, young men fathering children indiscriminately, widespread neglect of children who were growing up in unbridled savagery and lawlessness to despise their mothers and disdain men and all authority. As one child psychiatrist said, we were simply witnessing a breakdown in society (*Observer*, October 17, 1993). Surely there could be no greater issue to rouse the concern of progressives? Apparently, not so.

Those who dared state that in general it was best for a child to be brought up by its mother and father took their professional and social lives in their hands. Encouraging lone mothers to move off welfare and into work was now deemed to be an extreme right-wing position, even though work and family had once been the twin pillars of ethical socialism. The left now identified itself with moral relativism, the doctrine that all lifestyles were equal and none could be deemed to be better than any other. But the idea that a woman could now be both mother and father to her children, and moreover that it was her "right" to choose such a lifestyle, led directly to the hopeless plight of often inadequate women left to struggle alone with raising children while the men who fathered them were in effect told they were free to do their own thing.

I was as perplexed by this as I was appalled. I had been brought up to believe that the left stood for altruism rather than selfishness, community rather than individualism, self-discipline rather than the law of the jungle and the survival of the fittest. Now, it seemed, the left was playing directly into the hands of the ideological right for whom the free and unfettered individual was all.

The right said there was no such thing as society; the left said there was no such thing as the family. The right cut taxes and let the poor go to the wall; the left cut family ties and let the children go to the wall. Both sides were worshipping at the shrine of individualism. Yet this was causing a rising tide of juvenile distress, crime, emotional disturbance, educational and relationship failure. "Haves" and "have-nots" were no longer defined by economics. Society was polarizing into those who had everything – family stability, decent education, jobs, houses and a reasonable life – and those who had nothing – no family stability, educational failure, no jobs, no houses and no stake in society as a result. Children, I wrote, needed to be taught that personal fulfillment had consequences for others: "To brand this a right-wing perspective is an abuse of language" (*Tablet*, July 31, 1993). But branded it was.

Not only that, but while moral codes that put others first were being junked a range of taboos was being established around race, gender and sexuality. One of the most dramatic examples of the oppressive and tyrannical nature of what was now called "political correctness" (but should more accurately be termed "cultural Marxism") was to be found in the world of social work. I wrote about the "anti-racist zealots" who had captured the social workers' training body, the Central Council for Education and Training in Social Work, and had built into the social workers' diploma the dogma that society was fundamentally racist and oppressive.

Once again, it was not some right-wing zealot who opened my eyes here to the way in which progressive circles were snuffing out freedom. Robert Pinker was Professor of Social Work Studies at the London School of Economics. He was an old-style liberal who was demonized because he took a stand against this brain-washing propaganda that was corrupting social work so badly that countless numbers of deeply disadvantaged clients were being abandoned or thrown to the wolves.

Pinker saw very clearly that factual evidence no longer counted for anything. Social workers were being told they were not allowed to test whether society was fundamentally racist or not. Evidence was being replaced by political slogans and indoctrination. Through him, I learned of situations so terrifying that I could scarcely believe these were happening in England. Social work tutors who asked to remain anonymous for fear of reprisals said students had come to them in tears after other tutors had told them: "You're white, so you must be racist; confess." Students reported that marks depended on displaying the "correct" attitude on race, which meant challenging "racist" attitudes even where none existed. Conversely, social workers were becoming too frightened to deal with black families for fear of being thought racist; it was therefore common for social workers to say it was normal for black families to beat their children (*Observer*, August 1, 1993).

Almost twenty years later, when a gang of Pakistani Muslim men was convicted in 2012 of more than two decades of sexual violence against young, predominantly white girls living in children's homes in the north of England, Ann Cryer, a former Labour MP, said that complaints to social workers and the police had been ignored because they were "petrified of being called racist" (*Daily Telegraph*, May 8, 2012).

It was voices on the left, again, that I took seriously when they identified the moral vacuum at the heart of the welfare state.

Frank Field MP had been an iconic anti-poverty campaigner. Yet by 1993, he was warning that expanding the welfare system was dragging more and more into welfare dependency rather than helping them to live independent lives. What had failed, it was becoming clear, was benevolent paternalism and it was thinkers on the left, like Field and David Piachaud, Professor of Social Administration at the LSE, who were saying so.

I was listening hard to what concerned caring professionals were telling me: that children in shattered families living on welfare benefits and with no fathers around possessed mountain bikes and video recorders, and yet when they arrived in their nursery class they had to be taught to eat with a knife and fork at a table because they had only ever eaten with their hands in front of the TV (*Observer*, October 17, 1993). Ours is a society of deep poverty, I wrote, but it is not merely material but moral and intellectual, with the breakdown of marriage at the root of this impoverishment (*Observer*, June 5, 1994).

I was becoming ever more horrified by the illiberal attitudes and measures being promoted by so-called liberal circles. These attitudes seemed to me to derive from a clear moral vacuum. What was so distressing was the utter contempt the left was displaying for ordinary people, those outside the gilded cages of the intelligentsia. I wrote of the guilt and self-loathing that had gripped the left which decided that the middle-class was patronizing, elitist, narrow-minded, parochial and prejudiced (unlike themselves, of course). This animus had penetrated deep into our cultural institutions, resulting in a kind of "cultural cleansing" of the middle class.

At the same time, the intelligentsia was in fact exhibiting deep contempt for the masses by treating them as morons.

In 1995, the BBC *Programme Strategy Review* said: "In many respects the needs of Asian and African-Caribbean audiences are the same as many others. Feature films and music are important parts of their lives" (*Observer*, February 1995). It never occurred to the BBC that what it was thus revealing was its default assumption that black people were, in fact, different from everyone else.

Such views were surely themselves racist. Yet racism, along with a host of other behavior, was now a deep taboo. Racial prejudice was necessarily abhorrent, but the new dogma of anti-racism, along with taboos against sexual harassment, pornography, date rape, and a range of gender and other stereotypes, constituted a perversely one-sided view of prejudice or aggression: that it could never be perpetrated by any group that designated itself to be victims of the majority.

I agreed with the American thinker Gertrude Himmelfarb that this represented a kind of "telescopic morality." It disdained "bourgeois" values such as chastity, fidelity, or sobriety; it marginalized incontrovertible rapes by its fixation with the far more ambiguous "date rape;" it didn't worry as much about crime, which created real victims, as uncivil speech which merely caused offence; and it placed the entire burden of guilt upon the privileged, while giving the disadvantaged a free pass for antisocial behavior. Such *fin-de-siècle* decadence, I wrote, was now wrecking the social fabric (*Tablet*, July 1, 1995).

But I had still not crossed the political floor. Instead, I scorned the ideologues of both left and right. The fragmentation of the family, I wrote, had been caused by an unholy alliance between the economic libertarianism of the right and the social libertarianism of the left: the free market in economics and the social market in lifestyles (*Observer*, July 11, 1993).

The reckoning for libertarianism on both left and right was now coming in. The Tories had all but killed off public service with what I saw as the vandalism of the NHS, civil service and BBC, dissolving Britain's cultural glue. Work was essential to human dignity, but the left refused to impose an obligation on unemployed people to get a job rather than subsist on welfare benefits, effectively declaring that it was better to be unemployed rather than work for low pay (*Observer*, June 19, 1994).

Both the state and the market had failed. On the left was social license; on the right, worship of individual profit, withdrawal of collective responsibility, and the identification of citizens with consumers. Youth culture was glorifying nihilism and violence, parents were junking both authority and parenting, teachers were repudiating authority and refusing to stand in for parents. Discipline was now frowned upon and punishment was taboo. Love had been turned into an expression of self-interest. Children were being told they could choose whether to have sex or take drugs. Deviancy, in the form of divorce or out-of-wedlock births, was now treated as normal; the traditional family, which had previously been considered normal, was now treated as a pathology that hid systemic abuse behind a respectable facade (*Observer*, June 4, 1996).

On the right, however, the obsession with market forces had reduced public life to an arid and brutal utilitarianism (*Observer*, January 9, 1994). The Tories believed self-interest was the route to happiness and the market was the panacea for every ill. This was why the "back to basics" initiative in the early 1990s, the attempt to restore basic standards to education that almost immediately morphed into an attack on sexual license, was such a disaster. It was not so much that that ministers themselves were being outed for their sexual peccadilloes but that John Major, the Prime Minister, wouldn't rule such behavior out of order. He seemed to be paralyzed by the fear of being branded "judgmental." Much later, he too was revealed to have been "playing away from home" with Edwina Currie MP.

Values such as duty, honesty or responsibility were being abandoned by the "anarchic libertarians" of the Tory party no less than the left. In 1994 I wrote: "The ground to be seized is that conservative ground. It is a space that was once filled by ethical socialism" (*Observer*, January 23, 1994). And I lamented the prevalence of ideologies – dogmatic "isms" – which drove out reason itself through the way in which they blinded people to reality. "Away with meaningless labels of left and right," I wrote; "we need an ism to end all isms" (*Observer*, July 4, 1993).

Fat chance! A creed I thought was supposed to represent tolerance instead disseminated intolerance. Those who were ostensibly committed to helping the oppressed had themselves become oppressive. Dissent from these prevailing orthodoxies was being suppressed through professional and social ostracism. The doctrine of non-judgmentalism meant no judgments at all – except for the savage judgment damning anyone who was judgmental. Language was being rewritten accordingly and certain words banned from use.

Trying to explain all this, I suggested that, during the long years when Margaret Thatcher had dominated British politics, left-wingers who found themselves excluded from much of the public sphere had trained their guns instead on the private sphere of personal behavior. Intent on establishing what seemed to be nothing less than a dictatorship of virtue, they were clearly following the path founded in the eighteenth century by Jean-Jacques Rousseau in "forcing people to be free," the formula for a witch-hunt.

For saying such things, I found myself fingered as the very worst witch. What I had written was turning up in distorted form in vituperative articles in the press. Told to my face I had become a reactionary fellow-traveler of the right, I was branded a "moralizer," which appeared to be a term of abuse. Clearly the only thing to be now was an "amoralizer," or maybe "immoralizer" (*The Spectator*, September 17, 1994).

Most of the time, those hurling such insults provided no contrary evidence or even arguments, just blanket denials and gratuitous abuse. Where some attempt was made to provide a reasoned argument, it consisted merely of parroting research that could swiftly be shown to be full of holes. On the issue of man-made global warming, there was no shortage of this kind of ammunition against my position. On that issue, I was also told repeatedly that as I was not a scientist myself I had no right even to speak about the subject, let alone expect to be taken seriously.

Of course, this was egregiously to misunderstand the role of a journalist. As on so many other topics on which I had no specialist expertise, I went to those who did. From these scientists I discovered first that, far from the warmists' contention that "the science was settled" and that all but a few Big Oil-financed cranks endorsed the inconvenient truth of man-made global warming, dozens of the most distinguished scientists in their field thought on the contrary that the whole thing was a scam. From them I learned facts about climate that, as with any other issue, I constantly tested out for consistency, logic, reasonableness and supporting evidence. It was on the basis of all this that I concluded that the claims made by the warmists had no reputable basis in science. Worse still, I discovered, not least from scientists who had themselves been involved with the Intergovernmental Panel on Climate Change, that some of the most fundamental research underpinning the theory was simply fraudulent.

In other words, on this, as on every other topic, I was doing what I had done ever since starting out in journalism: following the evidence where it led, and only then reaching a conclusion.

But did I ever doubt myself? Of course I did, and still do. One of the many complaints bowled in my direction is that "you always seem so sure of yourself" – a grievous fault, obviously, to those for whom non-judgmental and ineffectual hand-wringing is the only acceptable, indeed virtuous, position.

In any event, this is once again to misunderstand the nature of the exercise. People confuse the strength of my views having reached a conclusion – that mass fatherlessness is causing untold harm, that educational orthodoxies are trapping the poor in disadvantage, that the man-made global warming scam has hoodwinked millions and cost billions – with the manner in which I reach that conclusion.

Of course I wondered whether I was wrong. How could I fail to do so, when so many seemed to be so sure that I was? How indeed could I be right, when I appeared to be so out of step with received wisdom? The risks of taking such a stand, moreover, are nerve-racking. The higher you stick your head above the parapet, the greater the danger that it will be blown off. All I could do was return to the evidence, check and re-check with new sources, constantly test out facts and logic, and try to keep an open mind.

For sure, sometimes I have got it wrong. After all, since I did come to the conclusion that my entire worldview in my early years was wrong I can hardly be accused of never changing my mind. But without wishing to sound boastful, I believe that on issue after issue where the evidence is now finally in, on education, family breakdown, multiculturalism, human rights law, the European Union, the effects of cannabis, and yes, man-made global warming, I have been proved right.

There is also another side-effect of enduring so much abuse. Eventually, the insults start losing their power. Once you have been called reactionary, right-wing, far-right, extreme-right, ultra-right, fascist, racist, Nazi, Holocaust-shroud-waver, warmonger, insane, and extreme right-wing insane racist warmongering Holocaust-shroud-waving Jew, what else can they throw at you?

Chapter 11

ALL MUST HAVE PRIZES

In 1996, I published a book analyzing what had happened to British education. It was called *All Must Have Prizes*. The title was drawn from the caucus race in Lewis Carroll's *Alice in Wonderland*, where the dodo announces that "everybody has won, and all must have prizes."

In this book, I wrote that education standards had not only plummeted but education itself had been redefined. It was no longer the transmission of knowledge and culture, but a process of self-discovery by "autonomous meaning-makers" – once known as pupils. This self-destructive process could only be understood in the context of a country and a society which had become radically demoralized. The ideological dogmas behind the unraveling of education were also eroding family life and the moral codes that kept civilized society together, replacing these by the "no blame, no shame, no pain society."

Respect for authority both in and outside the classroom had collapsed. Knowledge had given way to creativity and spontaneity. Literacy had been redefined as un-reading. The essay had been supplanted by the imaginative story, replacing teaching children to think by allowing them to imagine.

Teaching the rules of grammar or math was frowned upon for stifling a child's innate creativity. Right and wrong answers were no longer distinguished from each other; relativism reigned instead, and children were told to make it up as they went along.

Beneath the resistance to structured reading schemes on the grounds that these separated children into sheep and goats and thus destroyed children's "self-esteem" lay a far more ideological agenda. The New Literacy, which substituted listening, memorizing and guesswork for being taught to decode the print on a page, encouraged the use of English teaching to "empower" children to correct social inequalities. Teaching children to read was apparently an injustice against working-class students. Children were empowered, it seemed, by "making their own meaning." So correcting children's mistakes was an illegitimate exercise of power. The classic 1985 teacher-training text *Read with Me* proposed teaching reading in such a way that children would "catch it like a cough" (John Willinsky, *The New Literacy*, Routledge, 1994; Liz Waterland, *Read with Me*, Thimble Press, 1985).

The outcome was a Lewis Carroll world in which the failure of a child to learn to read was glorified as evidence of success. The result was mass functional illiteracy among school leavers, and associated behavioral problems by pupils excluded from classroom life through their inability to read. Even universities were forced to provide remedial courses for undergraduates to compensate for the gross inadequacies of the education system.

Most teachers, I wrote, were unaware that they were the unwitting troops of a cultural revolution, being now taught to teach according to doctrines whose core aim was to subvert the fundamental tenets of Western society. A generation of activists had captured academia and, in accordance with the strategy of cultural subversion advocated by Antonin Gramsci, had successfully suborned education to a far-left agenda.

My book caused a sensation. The *Observer* received one of its largest and angriest batch of letters to the editor after it published excerpts, so much so that it devoted an entire page to publishing some of the reaction. I was accused of "paranoia," "disreputable journalism," "tunnel vision," "unfounded prejudices" and "a mischievous misuse of journalistic power." The children's author Michael Rosen sneered: "It must be nice being Melanie Phillips believing in phonics, when 'phonics' itself can't be spelt phonically," and "when you're as knowledgeable as that, you don't have to mess around with silly things like evidence" (*Observer*, September 15, 1996).

All Must Have Prizes was described as the "worst written book of the year" (*LRB*, October 3, 1996), "a farrago of ignorance and inaccuracy," (Colin McCabe, *New Statesman*) "monomania" (Terry Eagleton, *Observer*, September 29, 1996), "outstanding tripe" and a "reactionary diatribe" (Lucy Kellaway, *Financial Times*, September 28, 1996). The *London Review of Books* lamented "The great Melanie Phillips disaster." The former Senior Chief Inspector of Schools, Professor Eric Bolton, sprayed epithets around his review such as "hyperbole," "tendentious," "vituperative," "absurd scenario," and "beneath contempt." Professor Ted Wragg, having sneered at its "selective and anecdotal nature" followed by a "lame solution," reported someone he described as a "fat bloke in pub" pronouncing "This is crap by anybody's standards" (*Independent*, September 13, 1996).

Wragg's additional implication that I had selectively cooked the evidence and had relied upon apparently nonexistent sources was so egregious that I wrote an article in the *Independent* the following day in which I pointed out the copious referenced and footnoted evidence in the book (*Independent*, September 13, 1996). Nevertheless, Professor John Sutherland spat: "It's a nice question what is most offensive about this book: the author's ignorance of her subject, the laziness of her methods or the arrogance of her pronouncements" (*London Review of Books*, October 3, 1996). So all the teachers, education psychologists, government inspectors, university professors, politicians, civil servants, parents and pupils to whom I had spoken or whom I was reporting, and all the educational texts and research reports I had read, were apparently not evidence but merely "anecdote" and "tittle-tattle." None of the evidence I produced from these sources was debated; it was merely denied.

Of course, the contempt for the real world displayed by these critics amply proved my point. As one reviewer noted, the mere mention of my name produced "knee-jerk reactions of vitriol" from most socialists of his acquaintance. But as he thoughtfully observed, what I was actually questioning was what being left-wing now meant. It was no longer about redistributing power and wealth from the few to the many; instead it was about pushing ideas stemming from the Romantic reaction to the Enlightenment. While entering some reservations, he agreed with my overall indictment of the loss of morality and responsibility, national self-confidence and purpose (*Chartist*, March-April 1997).

The great battle over education had one unexpected spin-off. For some years during the nineties I was in fairly regular touch with the Prince of Wales. The common cause between us was the state of British education, and on this issue we had many cordial and fascinating conversations. I have never broken his confidence in revealing what he said to me during those encounters, and I never will. There came a point, however, when there was a changing of the guard in his private office and I suddenly found myself out in the cold. I believe the reason was that I thought some of the education advisers now included in his circle were less than wholly sound and I told him so. Whether, as a result, I was deemed by his people to have become too difficult, I do not know; but from that time on, all contact with the Prince of Wales ceased.

My parents loyally read all my articles and books, but with increasing bemusement. They simply could not understand why I was now apparently siding with people like Conservative politicians, who were by definition a Bad Thing, against people like teachers, who were by definition a Very Good Thing. I tried to explain that left-wing people had changed and were now taking up positions that were harmful, particularly to disadvantaged people, but my poor parents simply couldn't cope with this. My mother took refuge in saying, "Well I'm sure you have very good reasons for thinking this" and then retreated into her knitting. My father would look at me, head cocked to one side, eyes clouded with perplexity and no little pain.

Chapter 12

THE BATTLE FOR BRITAIN'S SOUL

On and on I marched, straight into the guns. What else could I do? One explosive issue led to another. During the 1990s, the ultra-feminist agenda behind the willed breakdown of the traditional family became ever bolder in attacking its real target: men. It seemed to me to be driven by women who were declaring, offensively and stupidly, that men were a waste of space and that no sensible woman "would take one home." Such women appeared merely to need men as sperm donors, walking wallets and occasional au pairs.

It also seemed to me that the right, excoriated as they were for apparent heartlessness towards single-parents whom they were always trying to get off welfare and into work, were actually in an unholy alliance with the left over this issue. In January 1990, I had written that Mrs. Thatcher had struck a national chord with a speech in which she talked about strengthening the system for chasing absentee fathers for maintenance (*The Guardian*, January 19, 1990). I approved of this at the time, on the grounds that it was an obvious outrage that so many non-resident fathers failed to pay child support for their children's upkeep.

But within a few years I had radically revised my position. Now I thought that reducing the duty of a father to a purely financial role would itself undermine the married family. It gave a woman an incentive to have a baby and then ditch its father. It was also surely manifestly unjust to require men to pay for the upkeep of their children, when as often as not they were prevented by the mothers from playing a proper, involved, fatherly role.

Both Mrs. Thatcher's government and the ultra-feminists therefore seemed to be singing from the same bash-the-man hymn-sheet. At the right-wing Institute of Economic Affairs, I had a number of spirited arguments about this with thinkers who accordingly regarded me with bemusement. Wasn't I supposed to be on their side? Well no, I wasn't. They saw everything in terms of economics; I saw things in terms of morality, justice and rational responses to incentives.

In 1999, I explored all this in detail in another book, *The Sex-Change Society: Feminised Britain and the Neutered Male*. It was published by a think tank, the Social Market Foundation. This was because I could not find a mainstream publisher who would take it. A few years previously, my literary agent had warned me that I was being blacklisted by the publishing world and he advised me to stop writing books on current affairs. Nonsense, I said, and dispensed with his services. I engaged a new literary agent and reported to him what I had been told. "What nonsense," he said, "of course you can get published." Alas, it was not nonsense. So the Social Market Foundation, which at the time was run by Tories who had migrated from Labour via the Social Democratic Party and were sympathetic to me, agreed to publish my book.

In it, I argued that the roles of the sexes were being reversed under a policy of enforced androgyny. Women were assuming the roles of both mothers and fathers while masculinity was being progressively written out of the cultural script and men were being bullied into turning into quasi-women. Far from delivering greater freedom for women, however, this agenda was actually harming them along with their children as both family life and normative values were destroyed (*The Sex-Change Society: Feminised Britain and the Neutered Male*; Social Market Foundation, November 1999).

The response from the sisterhood was as apoplectic as it was incredulous. The *Daily Telegraph* noted with sympathy in an editorial, no less, that "Response by female writers to this book was venomous." Columnist Julie Burchill implied that I was suffering from sexual frustration. Another columnist, Suzanne Moore, suggested that I should "get out more." Yet another, Maureen Freely, wrote about my "bizarre gyrations over girl power." She asked: "Has she lost her mind? I'm afraid the answer is no." Since I was not clinically insane, in her view, I must therefore be a fanatic. I was apparently a "born-again social conservative, or should I say fundamentalist" who offered the "usual specious mix of biological determinism, skewed statistics, out of context research findings and wild statements" to express my "Savonarolean faith in the heaven that was the ideal fifties family" (*The Guardian*, November 5, 1997).

In the *New Statesman*, Geraldine Bedell was astonished that I could still call myself a progressive having written about an unspoken conspiracy to get badly behaved women to exclude men and thus undermine the family. Apparently it was my "judgmental" tone which meant I could not be a progressive and had the left "fuming." Seeking explanation for this upset of the natural order, Bedell told readers that I was a "true believer" whose "austere quality is emphasized by her fiercely short haircut and strong defined features" (*New Statesman*, November 1, 1999). Just imagine the feminist outcry if a man had written that!

For all the insults, there was still a grudging acknowledgement that I had a point. The Labour MP Denis MacShane thought the "fury of the attacks" on me masked the fact that "an awful lot of what she writes makes sense," even though for him my thought-crime was to be "anti-European" (*Independent*, November 16, 1999). William Leith, who felt the book was like "intellectual pornography," added: "Still, a lot of it makes sense;" and Claudia FitzHerbert found my faith in marriage "an oddly optimistic vision from such a cross and despairing pen" (*Daily Telegraph*, January 29, 1999).

It was around this time that a handwritten note went up on *The Guardian's* notice board that I may have been a woman but I was definitely not a sister.

While the issue of the family mutated into man-hating feminism, education mutated into the onslaught against national identity. In the mid-nineties, this battle was joined at national level when the head of the national curriculum authority, Dr. Nick Tate, tried to challenge the orthodoxy under which history teaching rejected the transmission of historical knowledge. It now aimed instead to prove that objectivity was an illusion, historical truth a chimera and that there was no established account of the past on which anyone could rely.

This was part of an agenda whose aim was nothing less than the dissolution of British national identity and the construction of a new, multicultural "narrative." It derived from the particular British self-flagellation over Empire and class, reinforced by the more general left-wing view that the nation state was an oppressive western construct that was innately racist and inescapably created nationalism, conflict and war.

Educationists claimed that transmitting a sense of national identity through education was "the new fundamentalism" associated with "the superiority of the British empire." They objected in particular to teaching classic English authors or British history to ethnic minority children. They said this was racist.

I was appalled. To me, this attitude threatened to deprive such children of what they needed to become equal and full participants in society. In an attack on Nick Tate in the *Cambridge Journal,* one education lecturer quoted with approval writers who questioned whether there could be any shared values at all. But to me, that meant freedom of speech, parliamentary democracy, the rule of law or monogamy could no longer be upheld (*New Statesman,* May 9, 1997).

I saw this as nothing less than outright nihilism which threatened to destroy the west. If all common bonds of tradition, custom, culture, morality and so forth were destroyed, there would no social glue to keep society together. It would gradually fracture into a set of disparate tribes with competing agendas and would thus eventually destroy itself. And as I was coming to realize, just about every issue on which I was so embattled, such as family, education, nation, and many more were all salients on the great battleground of the culture wars on which the defenders of the West were losing hands down.

As far back as 1989, I had grasped that multiculturalism was problematic and a threat to liberty. The Church of England was proposing that the blasphemy law, which applied only to Christianity, should be replaced by a new offense of insulting or outraging the religious feelings of any group in the community. This took place merely weeks after Iran's Ayatollah Khomeini had issued his notorious fatwa calling for the murder of the author Salman Rushdie on account of the purported offense to Islam given by his novel, *The Satanic Verses*.

Rushdie was forced to live in hiding for several years. But the Church's response was to surrender to terrorism and abandon the defense of the West by seeking to criminalize the giving of all such religious offense.

On this I was very clear from the start. Criminalizing the giving of offense as blasphemy was a "terribly muddled and dangerous" curtailment of liberty, since almost by definition every great faith that believed itself to be the sole repository of truth would give offense to others (*The Guardian*, March 3, 1989). And whereas the blasphemy law in defense of Christianity was hardly ever used, a new law criminalizing all religious offense would become a weapon enabling Islamic militants to destroy freedom of expression.

A foreign tyranny had put a bounty on the head of a British citizen who was now being forced to live in hiding for his life. You would have thought that all decent people in Britain would be united in outrage. Not so; in a chilling echo of history Rushdie's book had been publicly burned, with a number of Labour MPs taking part in this auto-da-fé.

As I wrote: "Labour MPs are nervously glancing over their shoulders at their Muslim constituents. It has been estimated that Labour could lose up to ten seats at the next election if disaffected Muslim voters organise behind their own candidates...Those who have faith should be free to practise it so long as that practice does not stifle the freedom of others – so no censorship, no book burning, no murder. That is why those who support the ban on the book, whatever their weasel words about abhorring violence, connive at the establishment of a medieval and theocratic lynch-mob" (*The Guardian*, July 28, 1989).

In 1990, I was aghast at the ambivalent attitudes of two Conservative MPs towards Rushdie's continuing plight. Peter Temple-Morris, chairman of the parliamentary Anglo-Iranian Group, and Robert Adley, chairman of the equivalent British-Syrian group, called upon Rushdie to make a gesture to pacify the Muslim world and thus break the deadlock over the Americans then being held hostage in Iran. I wrote about the "mind-twisting inversion of reality" and surrender of the British government to the threat of Islamic violence, with the extraordinary decision not to prosecute anyone for threatening Rushdie's life even though two prominent Muslims had stated they would sacrifice their own lives and those of their children if the opportunity arose to kill him.

It was an uncanny preview of what was to engulf Britain and the West in later years. More than a quarter of a century on it is clear that the Rushdie affair, and in particular the capitulation by the British political and so-called progressive establishment to terrorist blackmail by religious fascists, was a defining moment in Britain's surrender of its will to survive.

In 1996, however, I was getting another whiff of the disaster that was looming. A state primary school in Birmingham, where seventy percent of pupils were Muslim, started teaching Islam in religious education classes; a residual multi-faith class would be held for the rest. I duly noted that "Islam is the spectre at the woolly liberals' feast" because unlike other minorities, Muslims expected their host culture to adapt to meet their requirements.

In schools with a high Muslim attendance, there were already running battles over separate playgrounds for girls and boys, the school uniform and the content of the syllabus. I noted the fundamental dilemma of pluralism when a society's core liberal values were denied by a belief system it felt obliged to accommodate. Surely we believed that freedom was better than tyranny, democracy than despotism, law than anarchy? If so, schools had to teach a common culture (*Observer*, February 11, 1996). The alternative, prevailing cultural relativism directly called into question whether a common culture based on liberal values could survive, a question that is obviously infinitely more acute today.

By the late nineties, I was fretting over a country that seemed to be sleepwalking over the edge of a cultural cliff. Britain was in the grip of hyper-individualism, doctrinaire group rights, education collapse, and family breakdown. What had gone missing was any sense of a shared national project. "Instead," I wrote, "there is a despairing stoicism in the face of the apparently inexorable decline of a nation, the value of whose national identity can be measured by history teachers who resist the very idea that they should teach British history as an elitist irrelevance" (*TLS*, March 14, 1997).

The fetish for subjective values rather than objective authority was also elevating emotion over reason to an alarming degree. The country succumbed to a hysterical outbreak of mass sentimentality and emotional incontinence over the death of Princess Diana in August 1997, absurdly projecting onto her the sublimation of popular feelings of victimization and dysfunctionality. Hard on the heels of this apparent cultural nervous breakdown, the Tory leadership under William Hague announced that old taboos had given way to less judgmental attitudes and so the Conservative party would reposition itself around a new tolerance and inclusiveness on the family. With the historic values underpinning national cohesion, moral responsibility and the very spine of Britain's liberal society now under attack, the response of the ostensible defenders of that society was to buckle.

In 1991, I had decided to stretch my wings a little at *The Guardian* and venture out of the social policy arena in which I had been pigeonholed ever since I was a cub reporter. Along with my increasing concerns about the absence of moral seriousness on the left, I was struck by the corresponding vacuity of the Labour party that seemed no longer to know what it believed in. I decided that the Labour politician who most perfectly epitomized this trend was a young MP who at that time held the party's employment portfolio. He was personable and telegenic and clearly one of the party's Young Turks because of his cool attitude towards Labour's trade union paymasters. Beyond that, though, he had not received a great deal of attention. His name was Tony Blair.

I interviewed him at his home in the fashionable North London neighborhood of Islington. As he talked, I was both charmed and intrigued. He was winsome and self-deprecating and talked earnestly about a new type of politics, a synthesis of individual freedom and community obligation. I didn't really know what to make of this. What did it mean?

In my article, which the Guardian headlined "A star strong on telly but weak on vision," I asked him about the difference between himself and his Conservative counterpart. He gave a somewhat vague answer about how the unions were vital but needed to be used differently. I noted his apparent discomfort when he described himself as a socialist and how he couldn't really define the difference between socialism and social democracy. I observed that his views sounded very reasonable but I wondered about the absence of passion. And I described him as "the cynosure of the new model Labour Party...a man without a shadow, a man with no form, no past to live down, or boast about or betray; a Labour politician with no anger, no personal experience of hardship or injustice to expiate, a pleasant man with a pleasant family living in a pleasant North London house" (*The Guardian*, June 29, 1991).

The reaction to my article was seismic. Blair himself was silent, but the political reporters at *The Guardian* went ballistic. My crime, as far as I could make out through the shouting, was that I had no business writing about Blair at all because I wasn't even a political reporter and had thus written a totally ridiculous piece which made the whole paper look stupid. Or something along those lines. Around that time, I happened to go to a party where I met Peter Mandelson, who had managed Labour's 1987 general election campaign and was now the prospective Labour parliamentary candidate for Hartlepool. He already had a burgeoning reputation as the party's Machiavelli. I barely knew him, but he too started shouting at me. "That was the single most disgraceful piece about a politician that I can ever remember reading!" he stormed. "You know what you are! You're a yuppie! You're just a yuppie!"

I was as bewildered as I was astounded. A yuppie was a young, upwardly mobile professional. Wasn't that supposed to be precisely the kind of person to whom the new model Labour party was now appealing? And anyway, quite how had my article exhibited this supposedly noxious characteristic?

As for my political colleagues, much of their ire surely derived from the fact that I was not a member of the Lobby, the group of political journalists with passes to the lobby of the House of Commons and which operates as a closed circle bound by common rules of reporting. In my view, the Lobby acts as a secretive and unaccountable conduit for politicians with the quid pro quo that the journalists will not rock the boat. Indeed, if they did so their source of stories would dry up – a fact brought home to me when a Labour minister was complaining about the "ingratitude" of a certain political correspondent at *The Guardian* who had written disobligingly about the Labour government, despite the fact that this minister had personally fed him stories for use every Monday when news was thin on the ground.

But the explosive reaction to my article was clearly not entirely due to such professional territorialism. Mandelson's reaction was key. Even at that very early stage, it later seemed to me, Blair had been singled out as a future party leader. Without the secret briefings of the parliamentary Lobby to constrain me, I had unwittingly pointed to the fledgling emperor who was destined to be crowned and had wondered aloud whether he had any clothes.

Having provoked such a reaction, I did not expect to be allowed into the Blair Presence ever again. Nevertheless, I did meet up with him on a few occasions both when he was Leader of the Opposition and early in his period as Prime Minister. After he became party leader in 1994, he invited me to see him in his rooms at Westminster. By this time, I had already been engaged for several years in hand-to-hand combat with the left over the issue of the family. Blair's words therefore astonished me. "I think there's a hole at the heart of the Labour party," he said, "and it's called the family. I want you to help me fill it."

So I sat and talked to him about the crucial significance of marriage, the relative catastrophe of broken families for both individuals and society and the terrible mistake of providing incentives to young girls to have babies without their father on board. He got out a pad of paper and wrote it all down. I realized from this conversation that he shared many, if not all, of my views on this; but he knew he would have the devil's own job in getting such a traditional family agenda past his colleagues. For the first time I saw him as an essentially lonely figure, pitting himself against his party. My estimation of him went up.

Subsequently, as my situation at Guardian Newspapers deteriorated, I was emboldened to mention my predicament to him. Once again, his reaction astonished me. He told me he saw me as an outrider for many of the ideas he supported but did not dare voice himself because of the inevitable hostility of the left. He thought therefore that I might be even more effective outside the relatively small and entirely closed thought-circle of *The Guardian*, presenting these ideas in a reasonable and nonpartisan fashion to those with minds that were still open and thus preparing the ground for his own policies to be received with more equanimity.

This conversation left me feeling uncomfortable. I was taken aback to discover I might be used in such a way, even passively. I didn't want to be the outrider of anyone. I believed that journalists had to be totally independent of all vested interests and in the pocket of nobody at all, not even by default. I was sorry I had even mentioned my position to him.

I needn't have worried. The scales fell from my eyes at virtually the moment Blair was sealing his destiny as the new Prime Minister. During the 1997 general election campaign, I heard on the radio the senior Labour politician Jack Straw state authoritatively that the Labour government was committed to the rights of those pursuing alternative family lifestyles. In that instant, I knew that whatever Blair might privately think there was no chance whatsoever that his government would shore up the traditional family. On the contrary, Straw had effectively announced that it would now accelerate the task of destroying it.

I was right. After Blair won the 1997 election, war was waged within the Labour government over family policy. On one side was Blair; on the other was virtually his entire Cabinet. The Prime Minister lost. As for me, I regarded the Labour government from the get-go as a threat to the values of Britain and western society in general. From family breakdown to multiculturalism, education to welfare reform, human rights to the EU, I viewed the Blair government either as pursuing a radical agenda to undermine British national identity and normative social and moral values or selling the pass over its ostensible but meaningless commitment to shoring them up.

With the exception of one occasion when Blair was in difficulties over his policy on the National Health Service and in desperation called in myself and others considered to be part of the "awkward squad" to tell him what we thought was going wrong, he never spoke to me again. Whether he personally came to think that my political position had become too "right-wing" or whether I had merely become too toxic on the left for him safely to be seen to associate with me, I do not know.

Chapter 13

I FINALLY LEAVE GUARDIAN NEWSPAPERS

In 1995, Peter Preston resigned as editor of *The Guardian*. I promptly threw my hat into the ring as his successor. In view of all that had happened to me at the paper, how could I possibly have done that? In view of all that had happened to me at the paper, how could I possibly not have done so? In the event, as was widely predicted, Alan Rusbridger became editor of *The Guardian*.

On a couple of occasions during this period, the cultural establishment did nod in my direction; but in both instances, it was scarcely an unambiguous gesture. In March 1996, to the amazement of all not least myself, I won the prestigious Orwell Prize for political writing. The prize had been established two years previously by the left-wing political thinker Bernard Crick. Months later, I ran into Professor Crick. "I was away when the prize was decided," he told me coldly, "but if I had been there at the time I can assure you it would not have been awarded to you."

At around the same time, I was approached by a production company to make a TV documentary about the family, an idea which was being pitched to the BBC. The producer was highly enthusiastic and excited about the project. "We think you are so reactionary that you are in the very vanguard of the new thinking!" he exclaimed. I didn't know whether to laugh or cry.

Who Killed the Family? was duly made and screened on BBC2 to general indifference. In subsequent years, several other producers came to me with ideas for TV documentaries for me to present. I told them I thought commissioning editors would not accept a proposal that featured me. "What nonsense," said these young men, "you are so box office!" One by one they came back chastened. "Can't understand it," they muttered. But one of them said a BBC bigwig had told him he had been underwhelmed by the family film. What a surprise.

The uneasy calm resulting from my move to the *Observer* did not last long. The Sunday title was hemorrhaging money and *The Guardian* was complaining. After about a year, Jonathan Fenby was replaced by Andrew Jaspan from the *Scotsman*; after another year, with the paper's fortunes still not improving, Jaspan was replaced by Will Hutton, from *The Guardian* and the BBC.

Hutton was an economics writer with an engaging Tiggerish disposition that charmed most who encountered him. Under his editorship, the "Guardianization" of the *Observer's* culture was swiftly completed. Its previous tone of tolerant liberalism finally gave way to the malign political correctness of *The Guardian*. After Labour won the 1997 general election, Hutton's front page – of which he appeared to be inordinately proud – carried the enormous headline: "Goodbye xenophobia."

As soon as I saw that headline, a chill ran through me. For it was a declaration of war upon dissent, a sign that under Hutton any deviation from leftist orthodoxy would be demonized. And exactly what was the viewpoint which was being vilified here as "xenophobia?" Why, the belief by the Conservative party that Britain should remain outside the euro and resist the tide of further EU integration and loss of national sovereignty: a view that sought to defend democratic self-government against erosion and extinction by bureaucratic corporatism. My view.

Given the catastrophic blow that the euro was subsequently seen to deal to the economies of certain EU member states, people in Britain came to congratulate themselves on having had the foresight not to have joined the European currency – the position damned by Hutton's *Observer* years previously as "xenophobia," which turned out to be a foretaste of the hysteria by the Remain side after the British voted for Brexit in 2016.

My premonition at that time that my position would become untenable was to be borne out by subsequent events. As a commentator on the principal issues of the day, my column had always been showcased in its obvious place on the op-ed pages. Now, however, Hutton dispatched me to the back of the paper – not in the main news section, but thrown in with articles that were not only essentially frivolous but often crude and vulgar. It was a powerful statement that was painfully obvious to all. I had been marginalized and my nose was being rubbed in it.

In his jolly, back-slapping way Hutton repeatedly joshed me about the differences between us. It was presumably all supposed to be good clean fun, but behind the forced bonhomie I sensed defensiveness and anger. Indeed, on one occasion that anger spilled into the open when I wrote a piece about the EU, only to find Hutton furiously accusing me of having not only deliberately contradicted his own position but having referred to academic sources of which he had made clear he disapproved.

His outrage was as ridiculous as it was off-limits. The idea that I had expressed such a view in order to spite him was offensive and absurd, and for an editor to object to the sources upon whom a writer was drawing was positively chilling. So much for a "liberal" editor.

As the paper became more and more uniform in its hard-edged views, I found myself increasingly in an all-too-familiar position. At the leader conferences that I attended I was usually out on a limb, with the rest of the room apparently united in incredulity at the views I was expressing.

And during this time I badly needed some public support, for the campaign against me in the education world had taken a particularly vicious turn. Some years previously, I had discovered one solitary but important ally in the battle over education standards. This was the Chief Inspector of Schools, Chris Woodhead, who had gone to war against what he described as failed teaching methods – and who had earned the undying enmity of the entire education establishment as a result.

To me, his eruption onto the education battlefield was like the arrival of the cavalry. In piece after piece, I endorsed his views and supported him against attack. As a result, I found myself regularly sniped at in the education press and certain gossip columns that suggested there was something fishy about the uncanny similarity between Woodhead's views and my own. But this congruence of views was only striking because we both happened to believe that the entire education establishment had taken a desperately wrong turn. The absence of other voices in support merely proved the point.

I suspected that some of this sniping was being fed by those around the then Education Secretary David Blunkett, who seemed to feel personally undermined by Woodhead and who had himself written bitterly – and falsely – about an apparent conspiracy between myself and the Chief Inspector of Schools. The unpleasant innuendo behind the sniping reached its nadir in 1996. In an article in the Times Educational Supplement, which juxtaposed pictures of myself and Woodhead as if we were Siamese twins and claimed we offered similar visions of despair, Paul Francis wrote:

"I didn't believe it at first. There was the usual staffroom gossip, but I always try to ignore that. I noticed the graffiti by the bike sheds – 'Mel 4 Chris' – but thought nothing of it. Then I saw it with my own eyes: they were there last Thursday, sitting together for our cameras. Journalist Melanie Phillips and Chief Inspector Chris Woodhead are definitely an item.

"Nothing romantic, you understand. This isn't a tabloid slur effected through sexist insinuation. No, the link with Chris and Melanie is intellectual, but it's powerful and dangerous all the same. They're united by a common emotion – exasperation. Out there are these bloody schools with bloody kids and bloody teachers, and they won't do what we want. Except it isn't 'we.' It's 'I,' and what passionately united Mel and Chris is their feeling of uniqueness, their sense that they have been chosen, separately but simultaneously, to say what's wrong with English education and to put it right" (TES, September 27, 1996).

Eventually, the war of attrition under Hutton wore me down until I finally conceded defeat. There were rumors that he would soon depart; but I was finally forced to acknowledge what I should have admitted a decade earlier, that I just did not fit any longer. When the Rupert Murdoch-owned *Sunday Times* approached me and offered me a slot as an op-ed columnist, at long last I gave in my notice. "I suppose there's nothing I can say which would change your mind?" Hutton said. I would have laughed out loud at such shamelessly transparent falseness if I had not been near to tears.

And so, after twenty-one years, I finally left Guardian Newspapers and became a columnist on the *Sunday Times*. Soon afterwards, I ran into one of my old mentors at *The Guardian*. "I would never work for Murdoch," he spat in contempt, and stalked off. I was no longer even to be talked to. After almost two decades of being under this man's wing at *The Guardian*, I was now erased from civil society. Such are the principles on the left, the sole repository of unbesmirchable virtue from which delusional promontory of self-regard are hurled thunderbolts of disdain at those who offend against its shibboleths.

While writing this memoir I heard that a former colleague was, after all these years, still smarting from earnest advice I had apparently given him back in the nineties not to work for a Murdoch paper. Did I really hold such views then? Maybe I did, maybe I didn't. For sure, the past is a different country for me now.

Chapter 14

A VOYAGE AWAY FROM MY FATHER

With my departure from the *Observer*, I was not just leaving a newspaper group. I was also leaving my father behind. Having led him, a wondering neophyte, onto the cultural uplands I was now declaring them to be contaminated soil. Like my mother, he was simply bewildered. He just couldn't understand how I could have broken with the side that, in his unshakeable view, stood up for the little man. That must mean I was now lining up with the boss class that stamped upon people like him. Not that he said so in so many words. Paralyzed by a combination of love, loyalty and inarticulacy he simply couldn't have done so. If only he had been able to have it out with me as an equal! I might have been irritated, resentful, furious even; but at least I would not have felt as if I was abandoning him in an act of familial treachery. As it was, his crestfallen puzzlement pierced me every time I saw him.

What indeed had I now become? Was I now a conservative? Was I right-wing?

Everyone seemed to think so. I was now invited to meetings at conservative think tanks and even as a speaker on their platforms. Much that such people said resonated with me. They seemed to be refreshingly rooted in the real world rather than frolicking in the Neverlands of theory and wishful thinking; they looked soberly at facts and evidence and had an open mind; in disagreement they were courteous and did not resort to abuse.

Yet for all that, I felt they were just not my tribe. Stubbornly I insisted: "I am not a conservative." Some agreed I was not; they told me I was an old-fashioned, authentic liberal. Others said, when they had finished laughing, that of course I was a conservative; in what way, after all, did I differ?

But differ I did, because I was still a radical. I still believed that society could and should be repaired, that abuses of power should be fought and the vulnerable protected. There were still dragons to slay; the only difference was that the dragons had turned out to be the very people who I had once thought were riding alongside me beneath the banners of decency, truth and justice.

And there were profound differences of outlook with my new conservative allies. I was certainly not a free-market devotee. On the contrary, I believed that the obsession with market forces was philistine and destructive. It reduced everything to economics and thus corroded institutions and values, among them some of the most important bonds of trust making up the social fabric, that conservatives should have been defending.

My perspective seemed not to fit conventional thinking on either left or right, because the values that drove me were not political or economic but moral.

My beef was with a society consumed by individualism, and that applied both to left and right. On the left it took the form of libertarian social policies, destruction of all external authority and replacement of the particular by the universal and of the nation state by transnational progressivism, human rights and victim culture. But I also saw individualism at work on the right expressed through worship of the free market, deemed to be the panacea for all ills.

This was my beef against Mrs. Thatcher, a position from which I have not departed to this day. Mrs. T did some excellent things, the most important of which was her heroic attempt to arrest and reverse Britain's morbid acceptance of its own decline. But there was a hole at the heart of Thatcherism. Its eponymous heroine was no respecter of tradition. She was also a radical, but one who believed that anything other than the free market was a conspiracy against human freedom.

I felt strongly that cultures could not be reduced to a balance sheet. It was simply inappropriate to imagine that British institutions should all be run like Marks and Spencer. Mrs. Thatcher regarded the market-insulated professions as a conspiracy against the consumer. She was against inherited convention and in favor of competition. She did not acknowledge that intangibles such as trust and disinterestedness were not only priceless but rested very often on just such inherited conventions.

I believed that, far from saving Britain, the Thatcherites' utilitarian reductionism had helped erode still further the basis for moral authority and cultural tradition. This contributed in turn to the decay in integrity and competence of British public life under Mrs. Thatcher's Conservative successor, John Major, in whose administration, I wrote, "official deceit, dissembling, and disinformation are now so routine they barely merit comment" while political life was run by "placemen and cronies" (*The Guardian*, January 16, 1993).

These opinions may surprise American conservatives for whom Baroness Thatcher (as she became) was a political titan beyond criticism, and who think that anyone who criticizes her must be a left-winger and that anyone not on the left must be an unqualified Thatcher supporter.

In my view, that kind of polarized thinking represents precisely the problem that now so bedevils politics both in the UK and America. It is perfectly possible to believe, as I do, that Lady Thatcher achieved some great things but did other things that weren't so wonderful. The left/right argument, which forecloses any such balanced approach, simply wipes out any political space on which people can meet and discuss issues on the basis of reasoned debate rather than ideological name-calling. It also prevents an appreciation that the most important omission from today's polarized political debates, and which in itself can cut through many of today's paralyzing political confusions, is any acknowledgement of morality.

To me, the free-for-all in personal values was mirrored by the free-for-all of market forces. It was liberalism gone wrong, removed from the constraints that guaranteed a free and civilized society. I was therefore neither left-wing nor right-wing but rather promoting a moral position. But the left had vacated morality for self-interest. Spitting hatred and pouring bile, it denounced "moralizers" such as me as sour and joyless glums. Irony and self-awareness were never the left's strongest suit.

In 1998, my increasingly uneasy encounters with my father came to an abrupt end when he died, one month after being diagnosed with cancer. Although he had rapidly become very weak, no state care was provided for him other than a weekly visit by a district nurse. He was my mother's principal caregiver. Yet no agency would provide any more than the mostly untrained girls sent in by the local council to help look after her for just a few hours per week.

One Sunday morning, it seemed to me that he had become very weak indeed; he could barely struggle onto a chair in the flat where my parents had lived all my life. When the district nurse arrived, I said I thought my father needed nursing. "All he needs is some TLC," she snapped, using the common abbreviation for "tender loving care."

By sheer good fortune, my mother's caregiver that morning was Elizabeth. This wonderful woman certainly had not been recruited off the streets. She had been a senior nurse until a back injury forced her to retire, and now she worked as a caregiver for social services. Elizabeth had lost her entire family during a firebombing in South Africa's Soweto and she regarded my mother as a kind of surrogate sister.

She looked at my father and told me what I knew, that he was dying. "I will stay with you until it happens," she said. "I will not leave you."

In the early evening, Elizabeth told me that the end was not far off. My father was in some internal discomfort and we called the doctor. He diagnosed a minor stomach complaint and prescribed medication which, it being a Sunday evening, would take me some time to obtain from a pharmacy. Confused, I asked whether my father wasn't in fact dying. "Who knows?" said the doctor breezily. "He could last for several weeks more." Elizabeth raised her eyes to heaven. A few hours later, my father died in her arms. When the same doctor returned that night to certify the death, he had the grace to blush.

I was now entirely responsible for my mother's care. All things considered, she was holding up well. She was adamant that she wanted to stay in her own home. I found what appeared to be a good private care agency, and set up a rolling system of live-in caregivers. So started a new and increasingly traumatic phase of the relationship between my mother and me. But all of that took place in a different world from the political and professional terrain on which I was now so embattled.

Chapter 15

FROM CULTURE WAR
TO THE WAR OF CIVILIZATION

After the raging fevers at *The Guardian* and *Observer*, the *Sunday Times* seemed to me like a convalescent home. I continued to write about the anti-man agenda of the battered women lobby, (*ST*, November 15, 1998), the importance of grammar schools for true social mobility, (*ST*, November 22, 1998) the continuing undermining of marriage, (*ST*, December 5, 1999) the false dawn of freedom without duty (*ST*, January 2, 2000) and the myth of man-made global warming (*ST*, April 15, 2001).

No one at the paper was nasty to me. No one wrote barely-coded attacks on me in its pages. No one seemed to regard my views as evil or deranged. The editor with whom I worked, Martin Ivens, was intelligent, thoughtful and pleasant. Everything quieted down.

The truth was, the *Sunday Times* was too quiet. Like the *Observer*, it was a Sunday paper and thus lacked the frantic pace of a daily title. For adrenaline junkies like me, this felt all wrong. It also wasn't where the action was because it wasn't in the front line of the culture war. My place was on that front line. It was therefore perhaps inevitable that, within a few years, I should find myself gracing the op-ed page of the great warrior paper on the other side of the barricades from *The Guardian*, its alter-ego and nemesis, the *Daily Mail*, voice of "Middle Britain" and savage scourge of the left.

The change in my situation now was almost comical. I had left the convalescent home to find myself navigating the slopes of Mount Etna in constant eruption. The Mail was not a tranquil environment. And I was struck by its similarities with *The Guardian*. Like Peter Preston in his day, the *Mail's* Editor-in-Chief Paul Dacre is a journalistic genius. Both papers display an unerring identification with the attitudes of their core readership. And both are fuelled by moral passion, although each would define morality very differently.

Although it was clear from the start that there were issues on which the *Mail* and I did not agree, I quickly found that many of my views fitted its own like a glove. I seemed to be attached by an umbilical cord to its Middle Britain core readership. This in turn led to taunts that I was now "preaching to the choir" from folk who seemed put out to be deprived of the spectator sport of watching the left treat me as a coconut shy. But as a wise person observed to me, in today's lethal cultural confusion there was in fact no more important role than preaching to the choir which otherwise would become demoralized – in every sense – and would no longer know quite what song it was supposed to be singing at all.

Like most others, I had not seen 9/11 coming. Yet two days earlier, in a column about the decline of Christianity in Britain, I wrote, "Liberal values will be protected only if Christianity holds the line as our dominant culture. A society which professes neutrality between cultures would create a void which Islam, with its militant political creed, would attempt to fill" (*ST*, September 9, 2001).

One week after the atrocity, I wrote: "This is where the world divides. Are you for us or against us? Are you prepared to do everything it takes to stand against terror, or are you going to succour it by word or deed?" (*ST*, September 16, 2001) For immediately after the Twin Towers collapsed, I realized that what the West was facing was different from ordinary terrorism and different again from war by one state on another. This was something more akin to a cancer in the global bloodstream that had to be fought with all the weapons, both military and cultural, at our disposal. Yet in that moment I also realized that the West would flinch from this fight, because it no longer recognized the difference between good and evil or the validity of preferring some cultures to others but had decided instead that all such concepts were relative. So it would most likely take the path of appeasement rather than the measures needed to defend itself from the attempt to destroy it. So, indeed, it has proved.

In the following weeks, I steadily warned of the threat to Britain of Islamic extremism. Always noting the existence of truly moderate Muslims, I nevertheless also drew attention to the Arab and Muslim agenda to exterminate Israel, as well as the open Jew-hatred and group libels being published in such purportedly mainstream Muslim publications as Q-News (*ST*, September 23, 2001).

I pointed out that British liberal society appeared to have a death wish, and suggested it could only survive if it dumped relativism and multiculturalism and reasserted its Christian identity – and if it also understood that supporting the Jews was pivotal to its own defense (*ST*, October 14, 2001).

As time went on, however, I became steadily more alarmed by the way in which the appeasement instinct was turning into a real threat to liberal values. The government appeared to be caving in to Muslim demands to suppress any criticism of Islam by criminalizing "religious hatred" (despite the watering down of legislation to that end). The country seemed to be in denial of Islamic militants who hated Britain and wanted to destroy it, and who constituted an "enemy within."

In 2006 I wrote about all this in my book *Londonistan*. For a while, it seemed as if this warning about what was happening to Britain was to be published only in the U.S., where Encounter Books rose to the challenge, since every mainstream British publisher turned it down. At the last minute a tiny UK imprint, Gibson Square, came forward and published it. The book caused a sensation for "saying the unsayable" and became a bestseller; today, its conclusions are widely viewed as "prescient."

Meanwhile, attacks on Jews were steadily rising as a result of the demonization of Israel and the anti-Jewish prejudice implicit in the double standards being employed (*ST*, October 21, 2001).

Since the eruption in 2000 of the Arab campaign of mass murder against Israelis, known as the "Second Intifada," I had been astounded and appalled by Britain's reaction. Israel's citizens were being blown to smithereens in buses and pizza parlors. Yet it was being vilified for attempting to defend itself against such attacks, while support was actually growing for those who turned themselves into human bombs to murder as many Israeli innocents as possible.

This was 1982 all over again but far, far worse. In 1982, Israel was being blamed after it went to war to defend itself against genocidal terror. From 2000–2005, Israel was being blamed even while its civilians were being slaughtered. The eruption of irrational hatred against Israel in Britain and the West was now even more outrageous, more deluded, more obsessional. And there was also an unmistakable endgame in mind: the destruction of Israel altogether by demonizing and delegitimizing it through an unstoppable torrent of distortions, fabrications, blood libels, selective omissions, egregious double standards and lies.

At that stage, I still did not consider myself a Zionist. I had by now visited Israel, but only on two occasions during 2000 to see my daughter on her gap-year there. Despite the fact that I had observed the eruption of anti-Israel and anti-Jewish bigotry during the Lebanon war in 1982, I had mentally parked these disturbing events as an aberration. Of course, I knew there was latent anti-Jewish feeling that had so alarmingly resurfaced during the Lebanon war, but wasn't it ever thus at the extremes? As for *The Guardian*, well, this was just a certain upperclass type of the kind that one found in the "camel corps" at the Foreign and Commonwealth Office. Nothing new or too disturbing about any of that, surely? Nothing to suggest I would ever feel that Britain itself could come to feel an uncomfortable place for a Jew. How wrong I was.

A watershed moment occurred in December 2001 when I was on the panel of *Question Time*, a weekly BBC current affairs show with a live audience. This edition was being televised from

Bristol, an educated, civilized university city. An Israeli in the audience asked why the Americans could go halfway around the world to root out terror in Afghanistan when the Israelis were condemned for doing the same in their own backyard. Was this not a double standard?

Not at all, said the rest of the panel. Despite its citizens being blown to bits in buses and cafes, Israel was apparently guilty of war crimes and the indiscriminate bombing of apparently universally innocent Palestinians. And from the audience came the considered view that Israel was the source of terror in the Middle East, that it was responsible for ethnic cleansing and that what it was doing was as bad as what was being done to it.

I was stupefied by such perverse factual and moral inversion. When it was my turn to answer the question, I said I wondered why people had no sympathy when Israelis tried to prevent themselves from being murdered, and that the Palestinian Authority was a sponsor of terror and incited violence daily against Israelis and Jews across the world.

As I spoke, I was aware of a low hissing from the audience. I looked at them and saw disbelief and faces convulsed with hatred. I said Israel was the only democracy in the Middle East. The audience laughed unpleasantly. Worse was to come. A novelist on the panel, Will Self, leaned across the table. Where, he demanded, did my own loyalties lie? If Britain declared war on Israel, whose side would I be on?

I was most deeply shocked. For defending Israel, I was being accused of dual loyalties, of somehow being a traitor to Britain, just because I was a Jew (no less barbed for the fact that Self, too, is of Jewish heritage). If I had been a non-Jew defending Israel, that particular charge would never have been laid against me: the ancient, bigoted canard of dual loyalty hurled at diaspora Jews throughout the centuries.

For myself and countless British Jews watching the show (as they tell me even to this day), this was a defining moment. In that instant, I realized this was not some rogue set of attitudes. British Jews had been living in a fools' paradise during the half-century since the discovery of the Nazi extermination camps had sent Jew-hatred underground. Now this had abruptly and shockingly come to an end. Mainstream opinion had become infected by an animus against Israel that was simply impervious to reason and which was in turn legitimizing anti-Jewish prejudice of the kind that once would have been confined to the fringes of society and subject to condign disapproval.

And there was no doubt that 9/11 had fed the madness. Astonishingly, a common reaction in Britain was that America had "had it coming" because it backed Israel, and it was Israel's "oppression" of the Palestinians that was the cause of Muslim rage. It was as if the Muslim-on-Muslim and Muslim-on-Christian jihad raging through the world, not to mention the explicit Islamist agenda to conquer the West, just didn't exist.

With this shattering development, the twin tracks of my isolation on social and cultural issues and my isolation on Israel were finally joined. People were not just swallowing and regurgitating lies about Israel and prejudice about Jews. In doing so they were, in effect, swallowing the propaganda from the enemies not just of Israel but of Britain and the West – while treating their defender, Israel, as the enemy. Instead of understanding that Israel and Britain faced the same threat, the British, who were so conspicuously failing to acknowledge the undermining of cultural cohesion from within, had decided that Israel was itself the threat and that any British Jew who supported Israel was a potential traitor. And all this while Israelis were regularly being blown to kingdom come.

Just as my mother was succumbing to the lethal perversity of autoimmune disease, so in the political sphere my country was doing something remarkably similar.

I also noticed that in making this protest, I appeared to be alone. No other Jews were getting stuck in. Heads in the Jewish community were being kept firmly below the parapet. The BBC was coming to me instead to put forward Israel's case. I felt it was my duty to do so, but first I had to make myself better informed about the Middle East. So I started to read widely, to learn and to listen.

As I did so, I realized to my growing discomfort first how ignorant I was, and secondly, how shallow my views about Israel had been. While always uneasy about the Oslo peace process and the "two-state solution," I had swallowed the received wisdom that the Israeli "settlers" were preventing a solution to the impasse. Now I began to realize they were in fact irrelevant to the actual cause of that impasse: the genocidal Arab aim of destroying Israel. This was being revealed with unambiguous starkness by the "second intifada," the mass murder of Israelis which was the Palestinian reaction to Israel's offer of more than ninety percent of the "occupied territories" for a state of Palestine. Moreover, in pretending that the Palestinians were acting in good faith, Britain was conniving at their repudiation of international treaty obligations in a pattern of perfidy and kowtowing to terror that Britain itself had inaugurated in pre-Israel Palestine.

The more I read, the more horrified I became by the scale of the intellectual and moral corruption that was becoming embedded in public discourse about the Middle East: the systematic rewriting of history, the denial of law and justice and the corresponding demonization and de-legitimization of Israel.

The more I understood, the more I spoke and wrote about this; and the more I did so, the more firmly I now found myself pigeonholed as the ultimate outsider. Previously unevenly matched "for balance" against lefties on TV or radio panels, I now found myself similarly outnumbered on such shows against Arabs or their supporters. Formerly damned as "right-wing," I was now consigned to a fresh circle of hell as "Melanie the warmongering Zionist Jew."

In the *Daily Mail*, I wrote that British Jews were now facing a nightmarish vision. Far from bringing about an end to global Jew-hatred, the State of Israel was being used as a catalyst for anti-Jewish feeling which had erupted when the Twin Towers were hit. "Under the guise of criticism of Israel, Jews are being accused of running American politics, bankrolling Tony Blair or being disloyal to Britain," I wrote. "They are told they should be ashamed to be Jews, that they all stick together, that they have a murderous history, and that they are the real cause of world terror. Before September 11, British Jews thought they were safe. Now they're not so sure" (*Daily Mail*, March 6, 2002).

In the *Spectator*, I wrote that as punishment for the crime of trying to defend itself against annihilation Israel was being subjected to a torrent of lies, distortions, libels, abandonment of objectivity and the substitution of malice and hatred for truth pouring out of the British and European media and establishment. Strikingly, this was echoing the moral inversion of victim and victimizer by which the Islamic jihadis justified their attacks on the West. The west was all too receptive to mind-twisting jihadi propaganda because it had already repudiated truth, reason and morality in its own domestic discourse (*Spectator*, April 20, 2002).

The really striking thing was that this Israel and Jew-bashing bigotry was strongest on the supposedly anti-racist left. As I noted in 2003, what was going on was a kind of Holocaust inversion with the Israelis being demonized as Nazis and the Palestinians given a free pass as the "new Jews." Hatred of the Jews now marched grotesquely behind the left's banner of anti-racism and human rights, giving rise not merely to distortions, fabrications and slander about Israel but mainstream media chat about the malign power of the Jews over America and world policy (*Spectator*, March 22, 2003). And tragically, Jews on the left were at the forefront of this anti-Israel witch-hunt, enabling British broadcasters to develop the delightful new spectator sport of Jew-baiting by putting a pro-Israel and an anti-Israel Jew in a studio together and watching each rip the other apart.

This all got worse and worse. In 2004, in the wake of a relatively huge rise in attacks on Jews in Britain, I noted the following: claims by a radio reporter that the Jews might have "poisoned the water wells of Egypt" in 1947; a Tory MP accusing British Jews of dual loyalty unless they repudiated the policies of the Israel government; and a woman at a dinner saying to my face, "I hate the Jews" (*Sunday Telegraph*, February 22, 2004).

As for the monotonously repeated claim that such venom was not Jew-hatred but merely hostility, much of it legitimate, towards Israel, this was, to put it mildly, disingenuous. This was not legitimate criticism but a unique campaign of de-legitimization based on fabrication, distortion and group libel. And it was its unique qualities that identified it as yet another mutation of anti-Jewish prejudice. For this "oldest hatred" is unlike any other form of prejudice. It is unique in displaying characteristics such as egregious double standards, obsessive fixation, imputation of cosmic malice and blaming the Jews for activities of which they are not only innocent, but of which they are, in fact, the victims.

All these unique characteristics were on display in the demonization of Israel, along with classic anti-Jewish tropes such as accusations of clannishness, sinister and covert power, and dual loyalty. Moreover, in denying to Israel alone the right to defend itself militarily against attack it endorsed Israel's destruction. In seeking to destroy Israel, it singled out the Jews alone as not having the right to self-determination in their own national homeland. In claiming that Zionism, the movement for the self-determination of the Jewish people, was in fact racism, it struck at the very heart of Judaism, for which the people, the religion, and the land are inseparable.

One left-wing commentator took me to task for suggesting that the anti-Israel discourse was in fact anti-Jew. "What you have to understand," he said earnestly, "is that we are just so relieved we don't have to worry about the Jews any more. Ever since Auschwitz we've been unable to criticize the Jews at all. Now we feel that constraint has been lifted."

In other words, now that Israelis were being presented as Nazis it was, thank goodness, back to business as usual for British Jew-haters.

The wholly false belief that Israel is the regional bully in the Middle East, and responsible for the absence of peace with the Palestinians because the conflict is essentially about setting boundaries on land which Israel illegitimately occupies, is now the default in Britain. Not only that, but the sickening campaign to delegitimize Israel in order to bring about its destruction consumes British public life.

This includes boycott campaigns conducted by trade unions, the Church of England and the medical profession; university tutors marking down students if they don't reproduce Arab propaganda about the Middle East; fashionable plays claiming that Israel persecutes the Palestinians because of the arrogant Jewish claim to be the "chosen people," and the relentless BBC coverage of the Middle East with its disproportionate coverage of Israel, its failure to report its victimization so that its military defense is presented as aggression, and its reflexive reproduction of Arab propaganda.

To live in a country where no official voice is raised against this vicious and racist madness, where British Jews who defend Israel become "you people" and their loyalty is called into question, and where the only good Jew is an anti-Zionist Jew is really quite intolerable.

In 1982, I was told my country was Israel even though I had never been there. In 2001, I was told I was disloyal to Britain just for supporting Israel's right to defend itself, even though I had visited it only twice and did not particularly want to go again. Time and again, I was told to go and live in Israel because that was "my country" when it was not. I could never relax when turning on the radio or TV, opening a newspaper or going to a dinner party for fear of coming up against some libelous accusation or other casual prejudice against Israel or the Jews. And if I protested, it was made clear that it was I who was causing great offense to decent British people – among whom, of course, I was no longer to be counted, but was instead to be disdained and marginalized as the "wailing Jew." I had been made to feel an outsider in my own country.

Subsequently, the issue of anti-Semitism in Britain came out of the closet and started to be discussed as a matter of increasing public concern. The immediate reason was the already controversial, far-left Labour party leader Jeremy Corbyn whose open endorsement of Hamas and Hezbollah was held to have created a permissive environment for openly anti-Jewish remarks by other prominent party members. These concerns gave rise in 2016 to an inquiry into antisemitism in the party which was nevertheless widely derided as a whitewash.

In fact, the problem of anti-Jewish feeling and the animus against Israel goes well beyond both Jeremy Corbyn and the Labour party. It has been poisoning British public life over several decades. Jewish students have for years run a gauntlet of anti-Israel and anti-Jewish aggression on British campuses, as they have done in American universities too. Yet there was general shock and surprise at the open Jew-hatred in the Labour party, as if this was a total aberration which had started happening out of the blue.

It came as no surprise to me. What people still fail to grasp is the symbiotic connection between anti-Jewish animus and the demonization and de-legitimization of Israel. It isn't merely that the venom against Israel shares exactly the same unique characteristics as Jew-hatred throughout the ages. The connection is deeply rooted in the anti-Western, anti-reason, anti-truth orthodoxy that has gripped the British intelligentsia to such an extent that they are now incapable of acknowledging any evidence that challenges their Manichean world view. In demonizing Israel, they are incapable of realizing that, far from being the avatars of anti-racist virtue that they firmly believe themselves to be, they are themselves displaying unadulterated bigotry by articulating the latest mutation of the oldest hatred.

The real tragedy of all this, however, is that it means Britain doesn't understand that the interests of its own Jewish community, which remains conspicuously loyal to Britain, dovetail completely with the geopolitical interests of Britain itself. And this is not despite the community's attachment to Israel, but because of it. If Israel were ever to go down, Britain and the West would be next in line and with no defender in the Middle East.

The fate of the Jewish people is inseparable from the fate of Britain and the West. Rather than leveling the distasteful canard of "dual loyalty" at those British Jews who feel an attachment to Israel, the British would serve their own interests rather better if they were to be more like America, where the non-Jewish public overwhelmingly backs Israel as the guarantor of its own liberty. Israel is the forward salient of the war to defend western civilization. Although the British do not seem to realize it, that includes them too.

It is in Israel that the defenders of Western civilization are fighting the battle with courage and integrity rather than cravenly cringing on their knees. Until 2000, I had never been there and never wanted to go. Now it is the place where I feel most safe. I am not alone in doing so.

Chapter 16

SEPARATED AT LAST

My mother remained in her own home for a little over a year after my father died. It was an increasingly stressful time; she disliked most of the women who were sent to care for her. I listened to her complaints. Were they justified? Was she being badly treated? I was in and out of her flat all the time, but it was impossible to judge. Her complaints became more and more insistent. I became increasingly frantic.

One day, she rang very early in the morning and claimed that the caregiver had hurt her. It was when she said that the girl was listening in on this call because she had penetrated the phone system that I called her general practitioner. Later that morning, I went with this GP to my mother's flat. The doctor told me my mother was suffering from a psychosis and needed hospitalization straight away. We knew she would probably refuse, but if between us we couldn't persuade her to go in voluntarily she would have to be sectioned under the Mental Health Act.

The GP talked to her plainly, carefully and gently. My mother looked at me. For a moment, the rigid Parkinson's mask that had turned her into a stranger seemed to slip away from her face; in that fleeting instant she became my mother again. Tenderly, she said: "Is this upsetting you very badly?" I couldn't trust myself to speak. "I'll go," she said.

I packed her bag and we left for the hospital. As she shuffled out of the front door, she said flatly, "I will never come back here again."

She remained in hospital for several weeks. The psychiatrist told me her brain was riddled with lesions. "She cannot go home," he said. I was distraught. I knew that my mother's great dread was that she would "end up in a home." How could I possibly do that to her? Should she come and live with us? Our house was totally unsuitable for her; should we perhaps sell it and move to somewhere fully equipped for a severely disabled person? Even if we did that, though, she would still need specialized nursing around the clock. But how could we possibly afford that?

Thus, I agonized with my mother's GP. Firmly she told me that my mother needed to be cared for in a nursing home. For a variety of reasons that she carefully listed, it would not be in my mother's interests for her to live with us; we simply wouldn't be able to cope with her rapidly multiplying needs. Living with us was out of the question.

Suspicious that the GP might be trying out of kindness to give me an escape route, I nevertheless accepted what she told me. I found a nursing home I thought was suitable and that was prepared to accept my mother. In the greatest possible dread, I braced myself to broach this with her. I expected tears, reproaches, resistance. To my astonishment, she accepted it without demur.

She lived in the nursing home for nearly four years. To begin with, she fought it; she stayed in her room, kept her distance from the other residents who she noted in horror were so very old and frail, and insisted on being addressed as "Mrs. Phillips" rather than by her given name. But then, finally, she submitted; she sat in the lounge with the others, stopped noticing her increasingly disheveled appearance, and became "Mabel." I don't know which tore me apart more.

As she had become too weak to wheel herself around the building, I bought her a motorized wheelchair. She struggled to control it, and the home gamely turned a blind eye to the plaster she took off the walls. But when she crashed it into other residents as they were having their hair done in the salon, the electric wheelchair was finally taken away from her. And then she was stranded, totally dependent upon others for everything she wanted to do.

I was told by social service professionals of my acquaintance that this home was "as good as it gets." There was not a week, however, when I did not feel the utmost anguish as I relentlessly noted every so-telling deficiency in her care – her spectacles coated with a film of dirt, the flowers left dead in her vase; not a week when I didn't fantasize about spiriting her out of the home; not a week when I did not bitterly reproach myself for having effectively put her there.

In my sleep, I dreamed that my mother rose from her wheelchair and, gently smiling, walked again.

As her mind disintegrated, my mother gradually left me. In 2004, a few minutes into her eightieth birthday, she died.

Chapter 17

A VERY STRANGE OBSESSION

Over the years, some people suggested that the dislike and disdain I had provoked by my writing was itself evidence of anti-Jewish prejudice. For sure, there was probably always an element of that and maybe it got stronger over the years. But in the main, I believe that this was not the main driver. I think I became a lightning rod for the onslaught by the left against the foundations of western society. That onslaught necessarily also meant attacking the Jewish people, whose ancient moral codes underpinned the west. I think I came to embody all of those things; and it was made much worse by the fact that I was not only an apostate of the left, but was calling them to account for betraying the very values they professed.

In other words, I was a kind of permanent reproach, a bad conscience. The fact that I continued to write along these lines regardless of all the abuse hurled to shut me up seemed to drive them simply nuts. After all, the sheer scale of their obsession with me and the things they have said, in literally hundreds of gratuitous comments every year for many years, are surely evidence of some kind of disorder. A few examples, chosen pretty well at random: "The routinely insane Melanie Phillips"

(Caitlin Moran, *Times*, April 14, 2012); "spoof columnist" (Martin Robbins, *The Guardian*, January 26, 2012); "One of the Mail's routine monsters" (Marina Hyde, *Independent*, November 23, 2011); "The Daily Mail's queen of mean" (Hugh Muir, *The Guardian*, November 9, 2011); "the simplistic authoritarian commentator Melanie Phillips" (Dave Hill, *The Guardian*, August 17, 2011); "depths of ignorance and bigotry that can scarcely have been matched, even in the Mail" (Greg Wood, *The Guardian*, December 6, 2011); "Consider the rightward and increasingly scary trajectory of – ooh, shall we say Melanie Phillips? – who started out as a Guardian herbivore and now, like Bertie Wooster's Aunt Agatha, eats broken bottles and kills rats with her teeth" (Nicholas Lezard, *Independent*, December 5, 2011).

In 2003, *The Guardian* devoted a two-page spread by Andy Beckett to my "extraordinary political journey." Why extraordinary? Because of my "background, choice of subjects, and the quality of [my] anger." But why, he wondered, was I so angry and severe? And how could I possibly have left my *Guardian* "family" and ended up at the *Daily Mail*? His puzzlement only increased when he saw my "buttery leather suit" which made me look like "a left-wing activist who has somehow acquired a *Daily Mail* salary." When I briefly mislaid my folder of papers, I momentarily seemed "scatty and quite normal;" but then when conversation commenced, I spoke "in formal paragraphs" (*The Guardian*, March 7, 2003). Oh dear.

Another interview with *The Guardian* in 2006, following publication of my book *Londonistan*, which charted Britain's capitulation to Islamist aggression, demonstrated the unbridgeable chasm between myself and the left. Jackie Ashley, the interviewer, found that my "hysterical tone repels frank and thoughtful argument;" indeed, it was "like interviewing a human cactus." My "medieval self-righteousness of tone" was apparently exemplified by the fact that I ordered only black coffee, behavior that was apparently so bizarre and intimidating that poor Ashley was too terrified even to ask for a bun.

But it was an exchange which was not included in the interview which for me encapsulated the chasm between myself and the left. Expressing exasperated disbelief at my description of "a debauched and disorderly culture of instant gratification, with disintegrating families, feral children and violence, squalor, and vulgarity on the streets," she waved her hand dismissively at the window and said, "I see no feral children. Where are they?"

We were sitting in a cafe in Chiswick, one of the most chic and well-to-do areas of London. Of course there were no feral children there, I said in astonishment. But in deprived and shattered communities, in the north of England for example, there were veritable cultural deserts where committed fathers were simply unknown and children who knew nothing but abandonment, disorder and violence were indeed not just wild and undisciplined but lacked the basic connection to a civilized society.

How could Ashley, a *Guardian* journalist, not know that there were now two Britains, one that was part of society and another that had largely detached itself from it? How could such misguided complacency possibly be considered progressive?

Why, though, was I so taken aback? I surely knew *The Guardian* mindset by now. I am always shocked, however, by the sheer scale of the disconnect between left-wingers and reality. I am always shocked by the sheer impossibility of getting them to see what is actually in front of their eyes. Indeed, it is terrifying. For it means that they are simply impervious to reason. It means that the west will always harbor those who will repeat the horrors of the past. And that means sliding into primitivism and chaos.

Those of us who live by the verbal sword must accept that we have chosen to inhabit the world of intellectual combat and not be too surprised by the missiles that are hurled our way. But I believe that what has happened to me illustrates what has happened to British society and western culture during the past three decades. It helps explain what is otherwise very hard to understand and bewilders so many: that our cultural and political elites have simply turned truth and justice inside out and, with argument replaced by insult and abuse, taken leave of reality itself. I believe that the left has suborned the center ground by hijacking the language of morality, virtue and progress, and that all these urgently need to be reclaimed for the true center ground.

So do I feel well satisfied to be shot of my former comrades with whom I have fallen out so badly? On the contrary: the whole thing remains for me deeply painful. It feels like being excluded from a family because it has joined some kind of weird brainwashing cult. The rupture with the left feels like a very bad divorce.

In May 2012, I went back to *The Guardian* for the first time in sixteen years to be interviewed by Ian Mayes, the editor of the latest volume of the paper's official history. I had known Ian a little when I was on the staff. He was now not only personally as courteous as I remembered, but referred in passing to insightful observations that former colleagues of mine had made to him about my experiences there. Maybe he was merely being tactful to get me to open up; nevertheless, it was the first time I had heard that anyone at the paper had been sympathetic to my story. When I left *The Guardian* building that day, I wept.

So am I over my rupture with the left? No. But here I am; and I can only do what I have always done and follow where the evidence leads. Will I continue to wonder whether I've got it all terribly wrong? Certainly. Will I persist in trying to reconcile my dream of Britain's Jerusalem with my love for the country whose capital city it is? Without doubt. Will I ever opt for a quieter life, renounce my views and conform to the received wisdom back in the company of my fashionable former friends? Never.

The problem for Britain and the West, however, is not confined to the political left. In June 2013 I was again on the panel of the BBC TV political show *Question Time*, this time in London. Replying to a question about whether Britain should arm the Syrian rebels, I said the real problem was the Iranian regime. This was not only behind Syria's President Assad but itself posed the single greatest threat to the West and needed to be neutralized.

My comments provoked uproar among the audience sitting in front of me. In vain, I tried to explain the danger posed to the world by a genocidal Iranian regime in thrall to an apocalyptic version of Islamic supremacism. Objectors in the audience accused me of being stupid, bigoted and the like. My fellow panelist Boris Johnson, then the Conservative Mayor of

London and now Britain's Foreign Secretary, divested himself of the opinion that Iran posed no threat to anyone in the world at all. This even though the world was trying to grapple with the danger posed by the nuclear program being pursued by the leading state sponsor of terrorism, the Islamic Republic of Iran.

A few weeks later the *Daily Mail*, for which I had written a column for the previous twelve years, rang up and fired me. No coherent reason was given. My shocked colleagues at the paper told me it was because the paper's hierarchy had disliked what I had said on *Question Time* about Iran. I had apparently fallen victim to the blinkered isolationism and instinct for appeasement on the political right, which had produced an almost identical state of denial about the threats to the West as the blinkered universalism and sanitizing of Islamist aggression on the political left.

My weekly column moved to *The Times*, which to my relief seemed to have no such difficulty in hosting a range of divergent views. Nevertheless, the unholy if unspoken alliance between left and right – of which, in one of fate's little ironies, I had twice fallen foul – had left Britain badly weakened before its enemies. With some notable exceptions, the political establishment in general had become so demoralized about Britain's place in the world and the record of the West that, on both foreign and domestic social issues, it was often hard to see where it differed from the post-modern, post-moral, politically correct leftist intelligentsia.

If Britain were to continue uninterrupted in this way, leading the rest of the west into destroying the building-blocks of its society, I believe a venerable culture that gave birth to freedom and democracy and some of the noblest aspirations of mankind will crumble under the pressures from both within and without.

And that's why the Brexit vote was so significant. This was the moment when a western nation, beaten and bullied and bad-mouthed for so long, finally got up off the floor and reasserted itself. Many people understood this to be so. I have lost count of the numbers who said to me, on both sides of the Atlantic, that Brexit was the last hope for the survival of Britain and also for Europe.

A culture can pull back from the brink of collapse if it tears off its suicidal blinders in time. This can still be achieved, but it requires a recognition above all of the paradox that so many fail to understand. This is that freedom only exists within clear boundaries, and that preserving the values of western civilization requires a robust reassertion of the Judeo-Christian principles on which its foundations rest. And that requires moral, political and religious leadership of the highest order, not to mention buckets of courage.

So, finally, to the question I am constantly asked whether I am now on the left or the right, the answer is: neither. I am simply Alfred and Mabel's daughter, a Jew who believes in helping make the world a better place and a journalist who believes in speaking truth to power.

As I always did from the start. Only some of the details have changed.

About the Author

The British journalist Melanie Phillips is Britain's most controversial champion of national and cultural identity. Her weekly column currently appears in The Times of London; she also writes for the Jerusalem Post and Jewish Chronicle and is a regular contributor to BBC TV and radio. Her bestselling book Londonistan, about the British establishment's capitulation to Islamist aggression, was published in 2006. She followed this in 2010 with The World Turned Upside Down: the Global Battle over God, Truth and Power. Her first novel, The Legacy, is due to be published in April 2018. You can follow her blog and all her work on her website, melaniephillips.com.